Motherhood
Without Guilt

D1025886

Motherhood Without Guilt

Being the Best Mother You Can Be and Feeling Great About It

Debra Gilbert Rosenberg, L.C.S.W.

SOURCEBOOKS, INC.
NAPERVILLE, ILLINOIS

Copyright © 2004 by Debra Gilbert Rosenberg
Cover and internal design © 2004 by Sourcebooks, Inc.
Cover image © 2004 Stone Images
Sourcebooks and the colophon are registered trademarks of
Sourcebooks, Inc.

Published by Sourcebooks, Inc.
P.O. Box 4410, Naperville, Illinois 60567-4410
(630) 961-3900
FAX: (630) 961-2168
www.sourcebooks.com

Library of Congress Cataloging-in-Publication Data

Rosenberg, Debra.
  Motherhood without guilt : being the best mother you can be
  and feeling great about it / Debra Gilbert Rosenberg.
      p. cm.
  Includes index.
  ISBN 1-4022-0228-8 (alk. paper)
  1. Motherhood. 2. Mothers. 3. Mothers--Family relationships.
I. Title.
HQ759.R6368 2004
306.874'3--dc22

                                    2004012181

ISBN 1-4022-0228-8

        Printed and bound in the United States of America
            VP 10 9 8 7 6 5 4 3 2 1

To mothers, who hold the most challenging and satisfying job on earth, and generally do it much better than they think.

Acknowledgements

My unconditional love and thanks go to my husband, Alan, and my children, Jill, Lynn, and Mark, who love me and have supported my efforts to write this book, while never trying to make *me* feel guilty for the time and energy I have devoted to it. I also thank my extended family: my own mother, Dorothy; my brothers and sister, Steve, Gary, and Kathy; my brothers-in-law and sisters-in-law, Sally, Noelle, Alfredo, Susan, and Michael; my father-in-law, Connie; my late mother-in-law, Myra; and Sue Miller, my significant-other-in-law and friend.

Without my women friends and colleagues, I couldn't have managed to write this. Thank you Alice, Amy, Ann, Beth, Carol, Christine, Cindy, Debra, Edie, Hilarie, Judy, Katherine, Kitty, Susan, Sylvie, and Tamar, and all of you with whom I shared wonderful conversations, for understanding when I needed to write and not talk, and for listening when I needed to talk and not write.

I am also appreciative of my friends whose contributions have directly enriched this book. Special thanks go to Debra Landay and Jenny Kemp for helping me come up with the idea for this book in the first place, and to Christine Baumbach, Chris Bullock, Kitty Hall, Hilarie Lieb, and Sylvie Sudarnac-Studney for their specific observations, insights, humor, and suggestions.

I am grateful to the members of my new mom's groups who have shared their ideas about motherhood and guilt with me, as well as my clients whose stories and efforts at healing and understanding have taught me that we mostly all try very hard to do our best, and most of us do better than we think.

Thanks to my agent, Linda Roghaar, for her calming and sensible advice and enthusiastic support.

Thanks also to Deb Werksman, who has become more than an editor to me. Her involvement in my work has made me a better writer, and her thoughts on motherhood have been invaluable. I value her opinion, her editorial skills, and her compassion, and I know I have been fortunate to work with her.

Table of Contents

Introduction

Motherhood without guilt? It's hard to imagine. We seem to expect so much of mothers. We expect mothers to be beautiful, healthy, loving, kind, intelligent, thoughtful, and fun; able to ease our discomforts almost before we feel them; available when we want them nearby, invisible when we don't. We also expect mothers to be in loving and fulfilling relationships, to have great friendships, and to have their own identities, but not to interfere with our own. We want mothers to be youthful, but not competitive with us; to be involved in their own interests, as long as they don't get in the way of attending our school and extracurricular events. We need moms who love us unconditionally, who keep our homes neat and clean and attractive, cook delicious and nutritious meals, and don't ever complain. We want them to take pride in our accomplishments, but not to need us to accomplish anything; we want mothers to want what we want for ourselves; to love us, to snuggle us when we want to be close, and to let us go when we are ready.

I've come to realize that what we want for mothers is a combination of Ginger Rogers and Fred Rogers. Ginger Rogers, Fred Astaire's most famous dance partner did everything that Fred Astaire did—but she did it all backward and in high heels! Mr. Rogers, the beloved children's TV show host, was understanding, unflappable, and offered unconditional love. We want mothers to have the beauty, grace, and selfless responsiveness of Ginger Rogers while sharing the wisdom and intelligence of Fred Rogers. It is impossible to live up to these images.

If a mother tries to do everything "right," to be this impossible ideal, that means she is dancing along in lockstep to her child, holding her child close, or letting her child dance independently; loving her child and finding her child fascinating even when the child doesn't look or behave as she had expected, or despite the child pursuing interests that bore her silly, and always in perfect accordance with the child's needs at any given moment, regardless of her own needs. And if these goals weren't challenging enough, at the same time she is maintaining her relationship with her life partner, she is trying to be a good daughter to aging parents, nurturing friendships, maybe holding down a job, and keeping the house comfortable and food available. While she is doing all that, she is trying to hold on to her own identity, follow her own interests, seek entertainment, and otherwise figure out how to get along and be the kind of person she wants to be. Inevitably, all these goals sometimes collide.

Motherhood without guilt? Is this possible? I'd like to think so, yet motherhood and guilt seem inextricably linked. Mothers feel guilty about their mothering; they feel guilty that they don't always say or do the right thing. They worry that they might be neglecting their children, husbands, parents, friends, or work, or they use guilt to manipulate their loved ones. No one seems to have enough time or energy to give; everyone wants to make everyone else happy and still manage to live her own life. Women want to be good mothers, good daughters, good everything; they want to have a satisfying love life, family connections, friendships, and meaningful work. Juggling all these roles and interactions is hard to do, so when one area of their life seems temporarily neglected or less than successful, mothers feel guilty.

Women who are mothers tell me all the time that they feel guilty about what they have or haven't done as a mom. They worry that they've ignored, smothered, hurt, or confused their children, loved ones, friends, or coworkers, and they talk about how much they care about being a good mom. They try really hard, yet they frequently find themselves somehow not living up to their own expectations. *They feel so guilty.*

As a clinical social worker and leader of support groups for first-time mothers, I've seen that mothers seem to be blamed for everything. I've worked for many years with women who worry that they are somehow not being good enough mothers and with troubled people who blame their mothers for many of their current life dilemmas. I first started thinking about writing about motherhood and guilt when it became clear to me that almost whenever I've talked to women about motherhood, no matter how conscientious and caring these mothers may be, they describe feeling guilty.

I don't think I've ever met a mother who didn't try to be the best possible mother she could be. Regardless of whether a mother stays at home full time or balances a career with taking care of her family; whether her kids are toddlers, teens, or fully grown adults with kids of their own; whether she is young or older herself, rich or poor, highly educated or not, married or single—a mother cares about her children, and about how her actions and words affect those kids. A mother's happiness often is tightly linked with her children's well-being.

You could spend years reading all the books on parenting, attending classes to hone your skills, and learning techniques and the best language to use to help you mother your children better. The more you know, though, the more you are likely to feel guilty when you don't employ those well-conceived ideas. Although I often agree with many of the parenting experts (and I think techniques or examples of how other moms have solved problems similar to what you may be experiencing can enrich your approach to motherhood), sometimes too much advice or information can make a mother feel overwhelmed and incompetent when she is really doing just fine. I believe that mothers often know what they should be doing, but they also need confidence, maturity, support, understanding, and self-acceptance in order to do it. They need to know that sometimes even the "right" thing may not work, and that they are not responsible for everything that goes on, good or bad, in their family's lives.

In working with mothers and families over the years, it seems to me that the "best" mothering doesn't necessarily follow any experts' advice to the letter, but comes from mothers who are honest, loving, and real, from mothers who are in touch with their own feelings, who listen to their children, and who adjust what they do with their kids to fit the specific child and situation. After all, mothers are real people, living their lives and learning how to mother as they go along.

Most mothers, if asked, would say that being a good mother is extremely important to them; most mothers believe they act in the best interests of their children, at least most of the time. Yet, sometimes, we find motherhood to be boring or tedious; sometimes we miss the freedom and spontaneity of our pre-motherhood days; sometimes as hard as we try to do right by our kids, bad things happen; sometimes we say or do things that hurt the very kids we so desperately love; sometimes we get uncontrollably angry with our kids or our husbands and we behave badly. Even the very best moms—those gracious, calm magicians you see, perfectly dressed, toting home-baked brownies and clean-faced, bright-eyed toddlers to their older child's school events in between their volunteer jobs and presenting cases to the Supreme Court—even Supermoms feel guilty about some aspects of their mothering.

So often we feel guilty about our mothering. Sometimes when we do or say something we know we shouldn't have, that "bad" action is accompanied by so much anger that we *don't* feel guilty, and then we feel guilty about that. Motherhood and guilt seem to go hand in hand.

Most mothers really try to do their best, to do right by their children, but every so often, by thoughtlessness, in frustration, or through lack of understanding, they do or say things that have an impact that they never intended. Their own emotions get in the way, there are deadlines at work to meet, or they are just too tired to respond or behave appropriately all the time.

That's because even the most thoughtful moms, the most well-educated moms, the very well-intentioned moms, are human. They occasionally question or regret what they've done, said, or felt. No matter how much you know, no matter how many books about parenting you've read, the fact that you are actually a regular human being will likely result in your sometimes messing up, or at least thinking you did. Because we know, or think we know, what we should be doing as mothers, and whenever we don't quite meet our own expectations, we feel just awful. We feel guilty. So many truly excellent moms feel guilty because, as much as they love and adore their children, and despite the fact that they would willingly lay down their lives to save their kids from harm, they also sometimes feel annoyed, yell when they know they shouldn't, harbor hateful feelings toward in-laws, or struggle with their conflicting desires to be everything to everybody.

What mothers need is not more books about what they *should* be doing. They need more support for what they are already doing. Mothers need to know that their good intentions usually are good enough; that the love they show their children, lovers, families, and communities is appreciated; and that the work they do has value. Mothers need to know that everyone makes mistakes; there is no such thing as perfection; that their "flaws" aren't flaws—they're personality traits; that mothering is not a science; and that no matter how hard you try, you will manage certain parts of motherhood exceedingly well and other parts not as well as you'd like. Mothers need to know that their mothering is probably more than good enough, and that as individuals (as mothers, daughters, wives, workers, and friends) they are, without a doubt, and regardless of the occasional misstep, good enough. And they need to know that most of the time, guilt is an unnecessary and useless burden.

Rather than offering you another book telling you what to do to be a better mother, this is a book about motherhood and guilt and how to avoid feeling guilty. This is a book to take care of you and your feelings as you mother your kids. This is a book to reassure you that many, many mothers yell too often; lots of mothers agonize over their decisions about working or staying at home; legions of moms worry that they've let their relationships slide away from them; and many moms who truly love being a mom don't always find motherhood to be all that stimulating or gratifying. These are all normal, nearly universal responses to motherhood.

This is a book to help mothers continue to love being mothers and, at the same time, learn to be a lot more accepting of themselves as mothers and as people. Ideally, reading this book will help moms feel better about their mothering. Understanding why they sometimes do things that they know better than to do should help them change some behaviors that probably *should* be changed. Knowing that lots of moms question their own feelings and actions should help them learn to stop feeling guilty about things that are probably okay. Being more self-accepting ought to help them raise more self-accepting children, who, in turn, I hope, will have less guilt weighing them down than their mothers have.

Sure, mothers are blamed for most of the emotional ills of the world, but I don't really see the value of all these wonderful, hard-working mothers drowning in guilt. Guilt makes even the most talented and compassionate moms among us insecure and full of self-doubt. Guilt and self-doubt are neither productive nor useful—they eat away at you. I believe that neither guilt nor self-doubt needs to accompany motherhood so often. This book is intended to help moms eliminate unnecessary and inappropriate guilt, and develop more self-confidence in their mothering.

I believe that *motherhood and guilt do not have to be synonymous*. Parenthood can be one of the most enriching and challenging jobs of your life. I know of little else that engages the mind, heart, soul, and body as completely and for the rest of your lifetime as much as parenthood. The trick is to be able to be a mother and still get on with your life, to love and care for your family wisely and well, to know that you are a good enough mother, and to know that you don't have to feel guilty.

I want mothers to be able to go about the business of motherhood with a bit more compassion for themselves, for other mothers, and for their children. I want women to set realistic goals and have reasonable expectations of themselves and of others. I hope that mothers who read this book will be reassured that most of the time they are doing just fine, and just fine is more than good enough; it's great. I want to eliminate perfectionism and increase self-acceptance and throw in a whole lot more fun.

Let me first explain how I think about guilt. Guilt is the emotion you feel when you know what you "should" do, but despite what you know, you behave in an impulsive, hurtful, thoughtless, or careless way. Defining guilt this way makes it easier to avoid, because if you act with good intentions (if you consider your options and try to do a good job), you won't feel as responsible or to blame when things don't quite work out. Of course, guilt is not always completely avoidable because sometimes loved ones' needs conflict, there's no clear best choice, or your options are too severely limited. In general, though, guilt can be diminished or eliminated when you regularly try to do what you think is right, when you are honest and forthright, and when you try to be a good person. When you know that your intentions are pure, and that your actions or words are well-meant, it's unlikely that you'll feel guilty; guilt shouldn't follow when you've tried to do the right thing, regardless of the outcome.

Despite our greatest efforts, though, we all do things that make us feel guilty at least sometimes. Here's an example of a nearly universal mother-behavior sure to stir up some legitimate guilt: at the end of a long day, you lose your temper and snap at your kids harshly and out of proportion to the situation. You know better; you, as an adult, know that you should be able to control your behavior no matter what the provocation. You know that screaming at the kids hurts them; you know that modeling out-of-control behavior teaches them that yelling is an acceptable way to deal with anger. So you feel guilty, and that's appropriate.

Feeling bad, though, can happen even if you do everything that you think you should be doing. Despite what all the experts seem to advise, many parenting decisions are somewhat murky. What works for one child may not work for another. What fits your personality and parenting style may seem ludicrous to your dearest friend. Sometimes doing what's best for one family member isn't what's best for another. Sometimes, despite all your vigilance and good wishes, bad things happen. For example, your child doesn't get invited to a classmate's birthday party. You feel bad for your child, but it isn't within your control to solve this problem. You can try to support your child's developing social skills, but it's your child's problem (or maybe the other child's). You feel bad and powerless that your child is hurt, but unless you did something to cause the other child or his mom to dislike you and your child, feeling guilty about your child's situation makes no sense; feeling bad that your child's feelings are hurt does.

It's normal to feel upset when bad things happen, especially when they happen to someone you love. Most mothers want the best for their families, but they mistakenly believe that if they do everything right, bad things won't happen. When bad things do happen, they feel guilty because they believe that they should have prevented the situation, even if they could have had no input or impact whatsoever. Unfortunately, that misguided belief that we really have so much control leads many moms to feel guilty when they've done nothing wrong. It makes sense to feel bad or sad when there are disappointments in life, but sometimes things just happen.

I believe that moms feel guilty too often, and that knowing the difference between *appropriate guilt* and *feeling bad* can help you become a better person and a better mother (not that you are a bad mother if you occasionally do something guilt-inducing). Ideally, feeling guilt—that nasty, unpleasant, nagging feeling that you did something wrong when you should have done better—will lead you to handling a situation better the next time, and knowing the difference between feeling guilty and feeling bad will allow you to let yourself off the hook when you aren't to blame.

The chapters in this book reflect the major areas about which mothers frequently feel guilty. Each chapter focuses on an area in a mother's life that commonly leads to mother-guilt, including what you do as a parent, your emotions about mothering, how your motherhood may impact the most important relationships in your life, and your concerns about working and about staying home. I've used a question and answer format to make it easier to find the specific issue that troubles you; the questions include the wide range of concerns mothers have that cause them to feel guilty or just bad about themselves or their mothering. I've included the most common and also most universal issues that cause moms to worry about their motherhood. Sometimes stories about a specific mom's issues serve as illustrations, but I never use the person's real name.

The first chapter covers the topics most mothers may think of first when guilt and mothering come to mind: it's about parenting their kids. This chapter covers things like nagging, giving your child permission to do something when you think you shouldn't have, forgetting to do something for your child, and the like. It's about what mothers do or don't do for or with their kids: what is enough, what may be too much.

The second chapter addresses the feelings you have about your kids. In this chapter, the questions relate more to how everybody feels than to what anybody does. These topics include the worries moms have about being patient enough, about sometimes wanting to take care of their own needs first, and facing their sometimes less-than-loving attitudes toward their kids. This chapter is about what it feels like to try to be a great mom while admitting that sometimes your feelings about mothering are not what you expected.

Having children dramatically changes your marriage, so chapter three focuses on the many concerns mothers have about their relationships with their children's fathers. Motherhood and being a wife are not always easy to juggle. The demands of children on the mom as an individual often cause her to put her relationship with her partner lower on her list of priorities than either he or she would like. So this chapter looks at questions about how to stay connected to your husband emotionally, how to deal with having less time alone together, and making all the adjustments couples need to make to keep their marriages alive.

Chapter four examines what to do when having children changes how you relate to your extended family. Mothers feel terrible when grandparents become competitive with each other, a divorce causes some cherished relationships to end, or different values or behaviors of loved ones cause tension. This chapter seeks to help moms handle problems that come up when you raise your children and still try to maintain comfortable relationships with relatives.

Friendships also change when a woman becomes a mother. Chapter five answers the many questions mothers have about how to maintain and develop satisfying friendships when your children usurp so much of your emotions and time. Dealing with competitive parenting among friends, changing interests, and disparate priorities are some of the issues included in this chapter.

Of course, I couldn't write a book about mother's guilt without a chapter on motherhood and working. No matter how advanced our society has become, mothers who work, whether full or part time, still feel guilty about working. Chapter six explores how to come to terms with missing school events; accepting that you may prefer working to staying at home; and juggling your many responsibilities.

The last chapter is for those women who are not working outside the home, or are working very minimally. Although people assume that stay-at-home moms might not feel guilty about staying home, unfortunately, they often do. These moms worry that by staying at home they are setting a poor example for their kids; they aren't contributing financially; or they are bored. Chapter seven supports moms who have decided to stay home to raise their kids by addressing their feelings, too.

Each chapter starts with an introduction that can be read separately from the questions and answers as it gives more of an overview of how I believe moms feel about that area in their lives. The introductions include general guidelines to the topic, as well as a broader approach to thinking about that area of your lives.

It's my goal and intention to help moms know that most guilt is unproductive. Motherhood is complicated. You are trying to raise kids, but you are also living your own life. It's difficult to take care of everyone else's needs as well as your own and do it all gracefully. Most thoughtful moms struggle with conflicting desires or demands on occasion, but if you are generally thoughtful about your mothering, and genuinely concerned about the important relationships in your life, you will do just fine. This book will help you know when guilt isn't called for, when you might try to do better the next time, and when you might be feeling bad and feeling bad is appropriate. It should help you eliminate much of the guilt from your mothering so that you can have motherhood without guilt.

Chapter One

What Mothers Do

A couple of days after a major snow fall, the sidewalks in my neighborhood had been cleared, the snow shoveled into little mountain ranges alongside the path. I was walking down the street toward a mother and her son, who looked to be about three years old. The two of them looked glad to be outdoors, and the sun was strong and bright. The boy was roly-poly in his padded snow pants and jacket, hooded, gloved, and wearing snow boots; the only part of him exposed was his face, and he was smiling. His mother kept pace with him on the cleared sidewalks while he scaled the mountains of snow, which in spots rose a foot or more above ground level.

What impressed me, in watching this mother and son, was the connection between them. The boy was completely focused as he walked atop the piled up snow, arms outstretched to keep his balance. When his balance threatened to fail him, he would briefly catch hold of his mom's hand, which was always right by his side; he'd steady himself, release her, and forge ahead. I don't think he was even aware that she had helped him out; he was totally engaged in meeting the challenge of the uneven, frozen terrain and proud that he could scale, what were to him, enormous heights. I'm sure he felt only the success of scrambling across the rugged snow, unaware that he used his mother's assistance for a fraction of a second here and there. His mother seemed proud of his skill and independence; she was always ready to help him, wordlessly, but also to let him try, wobble, move ahead. It was a lovely example of excellent parenting.

I am reasonably sure that neither of them would remember that day as anything special. I remember it vividly, though, because it illustrated to me in the purest imaginable form what I believe good parenting is all about. This child was testing his skills and interests, and his mother was there, supportive but unobtrusive, keeping him safe without holding him back. It was his idea to scramble across the piled up snow as they walked. He chose the path and she helped him achieve his goal. They were both so pleased.

Of course, this example of excellent parenting was memorable to me because it is so pure. Often, parenting is much more complicated. Mothers do not always have the luxury of being able to follow and support their child's whims, and sometimes the whims themselves are more questionable. It is not always clear what you should or shouldn't do as a parent, and sometimes real life issues beyond the immediate needs of your child intrude, so you can't always do what's best for your child.

Mothers want to do what is best for their kids, even though sometimes they don't or can't do what they know they should— and often, they aren't even able to figure out what that might be. This chapter is about what you do or don't do with your children. There are innumerable books about how to be a good parent; this isn't one of them. Although this chapter addresses parenting actions, it looks at those behaviors from a different angle. This chapter examines what you do with your kids that you think maybe you shouldn't, and tries to help you interact with your children so that you and your kids will feel better about those interactions.

I believe that there are a huge variety of parenting experts for a reason: there are lots of good approaches to child rearing. Many ideas work well for many parents, but not everything works for everybody. Children and parents each have unique styles and attitudes, and so sometimes even the most highly respected and seemingly good idea disappoints. Time-outs, for example, are extraordinarily effective with some children and totally useless with others.

I prefer thinking about parenting as a process, and about what you do or don't do with your kids as best governed by broad guidelines. Most techniques—the how-to, what-to-say, or what-to-do suggestions many parents desire—are founded on excellent principles. However, parents often use those techniques incorrectly or take them to an extreme because they don't understand the principles, and so even "expert" ideas don't always work. Rather than a list of concrete suggestions for what to do as a parent, then, I think what good parents need is to understand those underlying principles; once understood and really accepted by the parent, those ideas lead parents to deal with their kids naturally, without the need to resort to parenting techniques or tricks. I believe there are ways of thinking about your children and interacting with them that lead to a decreased need for specific techniques.

Here are what I consider the very basics of parenthood. They are simple, straightforward, clear, and form the backbone of many "expert's" parenting advice. They are concepts rather than specific suggestions, though, as I believe that parents need to use their own style. Employing these ideas will not guarantee the prevention of any future misfortune, but should help you avoid too much permanent psychic scarring (yours or your kids). They are also good ideas for most of the relationships in life, as they call for honest, kind, and thoughtful interaction—behaviors that are always valuable.

My ideas of the principles of good parenting:

- ❧ Listen to your children and to your mate. Do not assume that you know what the other person is going to say. Pay attention to what your loved ones tell you and don't interrupt them. Good listening lets you get to know your loved ones and shows respect.
- ❧ Think before you speak or act. Sometimes taking an extra few seconds or minutes to think through your response allows you to compose yourself and avoid saying or doing something you will later regret. Remember, no matter how fervently you apologize, once words are spoken (or a child slapped) whatever was said or done cannot be taken back.
- ❧ Be consistent and don't undermine your own rules. If there is a family rule against eating in the living room, then don't *you* eat in the living room. If bedtime for the kids is 8:30 PM, then don't encourage new or wild activities at 8:15 unless there is a clear and well-communicated explanation for breaking your own rules.
- ❧ Sometimes, though, it is necessary or fun to "break" your own rules. Having a picnic in the living room or letting your kids stay up late to watch a lunar eclipse can be a great adventure as long as they understand that you are making a conscious decision to do things a little differently. Make special occasions clearly special, then, explain the reason for changing the rules, especially for the youngest child who will have trouble understanding why this time something is acceptable when otherwise it isn't.

❧ Be respectful of each family member. Do not resort to unkind teasing or making fun of anyone, especially if there is any question that the comments might hurt someone's feelings. What's funny to you may not be funny to the child, so consider how the comment or joke will be received before making it.

❧ Be honest. Most of the time, if you behave with integrity, lying isn't necessary or useful. For example, it's usually okay to turn down an invitation if you are very tired and just want to rest; really good friends will understand so you won't need to fabricate some previous commitment. When you lie or "bend" the truth, your children know, and they will learn that lying is an acceptable way to solve a social dilemma. They will also wonder if they can trust you to be truthful with them.

❧ Say what you mean and mean what you say. Being polite but clear about what you want, or don't want, generally saves everybody a lot of time and embarrassment and avoids manipulative behaviors. Children need to learn how to politely get what they need or want. If you are constantly evasive, need to be prodded to ask for what you really want, or say "no" when you mean "yes," your kids will learn to be evasive or manipulative and will have trouble communicating clearly with others. For example, if in your family, everyone says "no" when offered something, even if they want it, because they know they will be asked repeatedly and can ultimately say "yes," they will have trouble understanding that when they are offered something at a friend's house, they may have only one opportunity to accept.

- Be reliable. Follow through on promises and don't promise what you can't or aren't likely to do. If you know you are unlikely to be able to attend a school play, don't promise that you will be there. When something unexpected and unavoidable causes you to delay fulfilling a promise, explain and apologize, and do your best to follow through as soon as possible.

- Be accepting of your children and of their friends. Do not be overly critical or demand unreasonable behaviors. Your kids are just kids; they have a lot to learn. Keep your expectations realistic and your comments positive. Be supportive of their development, achievements, and interests, regardless of what they are.

- Love your family members for who they are, not what they do. Do not get too invested in their accomplishments because then they will believe that you love them only for being so smart, or so pretty, or such a great dancer. Then they may worry that you don't love who they are underneath, or won't love them if they don't continue to be so successful.

- Show that you love who they are, not what they do, by being interested in the process, not the product. That means finding out what your son loves about chess, why your daughter chose green instead of blue to paint the mountains. Instead of complimenting the end product, ask your child what he enjoys and why, or have her explain what she did, rather than focusing on the result. Accept yourself, your spouse, your kids, and your friends for all that they are, even if their interests or talents are unfamiliar to you.

- Understand that no one is perfect. Define yourself by your best moments, not your worst. Try to think of the things you don't like so much about yourself or others as character traits, not flaws. Mistakes may just show that you've tried something hard or new, and always present an opportunity for learning. If you can tolerate imperfections in yourself, you will be more tolerant of others.

- Tailor your parenting to the needs of your specific child. Some children want and need a lot of input, a lot of guidance, while others want to try things out and learn from their own mistakes. Offer only what each specific child needs and wants, paying attention to the possibility that at some ages the same child will want more or less involvement than at others, and that some children want more direct involvement than others.

- Use natural consequences to help shape a child's behavior whenever possible. When a child routinely doesn't finish his homework, for example, turning off the TV until he's done makes sense; denying him dinner makes no sense. When the consequences are logical, they have meaning to a child. Figuring out the problem and helping the child solve it helps children *want* to cooperate. Punishment, particularly if it is harsh or belittling, creates an atmosphere of fear; if your child feels that you will not love him if he disappoints you or breaks a rule, then he will have no self-confidence or self-esteem. Ultimately, you want your children to do what is right because it is right, not out of fear of punishment or withdrawal of your love.

- Do not blackmail or bribe your child. Do not threaten to make your child miss her best friend's birthday party unless she does extra chores, and do not use gifts or food to prompt a child to do what's expected of her routinely. When a child does something particularly well, or is especially kind, surprising him with a desired privilege or treat is fine, but gifts should not become the goal for being a well-behaved kid.

- Don't label your kids. Unflattering labels are bad for obvious reasons; calling a child ugly or stupid crushes his self-esteem. But even good labels can be harmful. Calling one child "the athletic one" or "smart one" limits his perception of himself, and sometimes makes him think that's *all* he is. Also, when a child hears too often that his brother is the funny child, he may not even attempt to nurture his own sense of humor. Labeling limits, so avoid it.

- Offer options whenever possible. "Take out the garbage right this minute" can become "Please take out the garbage before dinner; we're eating in an hour." This allows your child some latitude as to when he carries out the chore. "Would you prefer peanut butter and jelly or grilled cheese?" eliminates having your child dictate the entire menu, while still offering a choice you can both accept. Only offer choices you are comfortable with, though, or you will back yourself into a corner. Offering peanut butter and jelly or veal cordon bleu is fine if you are willing to prepare either, but not at all fine if one or the other is not actually okay.

- If something is nonnegotiable, be clear about it from the start. If everyone must go to the museum on Saturday, then say so. Do not ask, "Would you like to go to the museum?" if *not* going isn't an option. It is not more polite to ask that way; it's just sneakier.

- Do not put your children in charge of the family. There will be many times when offering a choice is reasonable, but there are many times when it is your prerogative as the mother and as an adult to make decisions by which your children must abide. As your children get older, you may want to consult them before choosing a vacation destination, but they should not be the ones to decide what the entire family eats for dinner every night, when to go to bed, what to wear to special events. Consider the situation before offering your children choices. If you've made an offer, be prepared to accept the child's choice.

- Say "please" and "thank you" whenever appropriate, even when the child or your spouse is doing a routine chore. Everyone likes to be appreciated, and being thanked or asked nicely shows that all efforts count, even those for which the person is always responsible.

- When your child intentionally misbehaves, when he purposefully and flagrantly breaks a rule and you feel that you must punish him, never give a punishment that is impossible to follow. Don't threaten to prevent your child from going on a class camp-out if it is required by his teacher. If an activity is required, not allowing your child to attend may be unreasonable. Also, do not suggest that your teenager will be grounded until her personality changes (as one frustrated mother did). A teenager is unable to change her personality at will, and the length of the grounding is overwhelming. Punishments lose all meaning if they are out of proportion to the infraction of the rules, or if they endure so long that the grounding becomes a way of life.

- Also, do not inflict a punishment on your child that inadvertently punishes another person. For example, if you don't allow your child to go to a special event with his best friend, that hurts the best friend, too. Keeping a child from visiting grandma disappoints grandma. If you must punish, don't punish people other than your child, too.

- Do not be emotionally abusive to or extremely critical of your mate, even if there's been a divorce. Children need to love and respect both parents and feel emotionally safe. Too harsh a criticism of your child's other parent feels dangerous to the child; they fear that you might turn on them next, withdraw your love, or be angry with them if they cross you.
- Do not hit, spank, slap, shake, or otherwise intentionally hurt your child physically. There are so many better alternatives to corporal punishment that I don't see the need to resort to slapping, beating, spanking, or any other infliction of physical pain. I'm not saying that parents who spank are necessarily bad or that corporal punishment is evil; I just don't see that it has any value, and numerous studies support this. I also believe physical punishment *creates* unnecessary problems; it teaches your child to be afraid of you, that physical violence can be an acceptable solution to problems, and that good behavior is desirable mostly to avoid pain.

I believe that if you can keep these guidelines in mind when you are interacting with your kids, you will not agonize so much about the details of what you need to do. Since people are so varied, and situations among families so complex, having basic principles to follow can be much more helpful than a list of more concrete suggestions. However, while some people like broad guidelines, some prefer more specific answers, and knowing what to do and then being able to put it into practice are often two different things. So, in addition to the above guidelines for thinking about what to do when parenting your kids, the rest of this chapter includes answers to the questions mothers have most frequently about many of the things they do that cause them to feel guilty.

How can I be sure that something I am doing (or not doing) isn't going to warp my child for life?

I wish I could tell you that there is some surefire way of knowing that whatever you do will be the right thing for your children, but parenthood, or for that matter, life, comes with no such guarantees. I have known lovely people who seem to do absolutely everything right according to the parenting experts, end up having tons of problems with their kids, and other parents who seem to ignore even the most obvious guidelines whose children appear to be well-adjusted, pleasant, and successful. Chances are that if you love your children and are reasonably responsive to their needs, you won't warp them for life. Be reassured that a lot more goes into creating permanent warping than just one or two actions.

Of course, some approaches to child rearing are more likely to destroy a child for life than others, so my suggestion is to be thoughtful about what you do as a parent whenever possible, use good judgment and a lot of love, and hope for the best. Treating a child badly; constant yelling, hitting, or calling the child cruel names; crushing a child's spirit; denying a child adequate food, shelter, love, or educational opportunities; ignoring a child; and only enjoying a child when he is performing or displaying certain behaviors are likely to be hurtful, and are relatively likely to wreck his life. Caring about being a good parent goes a long way though, and since you probably wouldn't be reading this book, or any others about parenting, if you didn't care about your kids, you're off to a very good start.

The best parents among us, I believe, are those who are well-matched to their children and usually adhere to some fairly straightforward rules of parenthood, like those outlined in the introduction to this chapter. Even the best parents occasionally have problems, though, as parenthood is not an exact science, and although we don't really want to believe this, we as parents do not have exclusive or total control over of our kids. Many other influences combine to make your children grow up as they do. It's unlikely, then, that any one specific thing you do or don't do will permanently damage your kids unless they were already on the way to being damaged.

Here's my suggestion: be thoughtful about what you do (or don't do) with your kids. Be careful not to hurt them, physically or emotionally, which means that you shouldn't hit, slap, or beat them, and you should be respectful and kind to them. Consider what is best for them. When you are feeling tired or crabby, take a bit more time in dealing with your children and try never to act out of anger. Take breaks when you are feeling overwhelmed so that your interactions are clear and what you do with your kids is about them, not about you. Take care of yourself so that you can take care of your children without feeling exhausted or resentful. Try to make the consequences of the child's misbehavior make sense to the child; extreme punishments tend to lose their meaning and therefore don't really provide much of a lesson for your kids and don't act as deterrents for future misbehaviors

If you feel that you have made an error in dealing with your kids, be upfront about it. Talk to your kids about the problems and engage them in conversation to try to solve those problems together. When you feel that you've made a mistake, accept that mistakes are a part of life. Own up to your blunder, work together to try to correct the problem, apologize, and move on. However, while it's important to forgive yourself and to ask for forgiveness from your kids, do not rely on apologies to allow yourself to get away with substandard parenting.

Don't be so worried that your actions will ruin your children's lives that you become rigid about decisions, or paralyzed and unable to make decisions at all. There are many, many ways to be a great parent. You have to be comfortable with your choices, and if you make decisions regarding your children with good intentions and a bit of forethought, you won't go too far wrong.

Accept that you and your kids are not perfect; you will all do things from time to time that disappoint, bother, or outright anger each other. The goal here is to do what is right for you and your kids whenever you can, and to accept that sometimes you all may fall somewhat short of that goal. Accepting yourself will help teach that to your kids, and will also help alleviate unnecessary guilt. Teach your children to be tolerant of themselves and others, including you. Help them learn forgiveness. When you are trying to be a good parent, you will undoubtedly miss the mark at least occasionally, but you don't need to worry that you will be ruining your child's life.

How will I know if I am doing enough for my kids?

"Enough" is such a hard word to define! How does anyone ever know when they are doing enough for anybody? Let's think about what it might mean to be doing enough. To me, doing enough means that your children are clean, adequately clothed and fed, have a safe and comfortable place to live, get enough sleep, and feel that they are loved. In addition, they have access to an education, medical and dental care, and opportunities to explore areas of their own interest. Nowhere does it say that all children need to wear the most fashionable clothes, go on exotic vacations, learn to speak three languages, play two musical instruments, and own the newest video games or computer accessories. Sometimes, I'm not even sure that such luxuries are advisable.

What children need most, beyond the essentials of living a reasonably healthy and safe life, is appropriate affection, attention, and nurturing from loved ones. They need to know that you are thrilled that they exist, that you find them, usually, pretty fascinating, and that you take pleasure in their figuring out who they are and what they want to do with their lives. They need to feel that their choices and behaviors, regardless of whether or not they choose for themselves what you would have chosen for them, will be acceptable to you, and they want to feel that whatever reasonable choices they make will be met with joy and approval, and not disdain.

You are doing enough for your kids if you offer them safety, love, and the opportunity to find out who they are, what they enjoy, and at what they excel. Forcing them to take piano lessons will be pointless and perhaps even damaging if they have no interest in the piano themselves, while denying them piano lessons, if the piano is their passion, will be devastating. The idea is to nurture the children in your life, not to shower them with stuff or opportunities that they cannot appreciate, or might even resent.

"Enough" has nothing to do with how you were raised or what you wished you had growing up. "Enough" really means providing your children with an environment that feels physically and emotionally safe, and the opportunity for each child to explore and develop his or her own interests and talents. Fortunately, it doesn't take a lot of money to do enough for your kids. The hardest part is to figure out what your child truly needs, to offer support and guidance without pressure, and to avoid the temptation either to give everything to and to do everything for your children, or to allow your children so much freedom and acceptance that they don't learn that their choices will always have consequences.

Don't worry too much about doing enough for your kids, despite living in a world where value is often measured in concrete terms. Do what seems right for you and your children, do not compete with your neighbors, relatives, or friends, and do not confuse your children's successes and failures with your own. Listen to your children when they talk to you, and watch their behaviors when they don't. Be tuned in to who your kids are as individuals and fill their needs as you understand them and deem them appropriate. Do what you can, love your children, honor their uniqueness, and enjoy them. This is much harder to do than simply making sure that their clothes are stylish, they go to the "right" schools, or that they participate in the "right" activities. But it will be enough.

I thought my parents were wonderful, but despite trying to do just what they did, their approach to child rearing doesn't seem to be working. What's going wrong?

My parents were just awful, so I'm trying to be very different with my kids. Yet sometimes I find the same words coming out of my mouth. How can I avoid duplicating their mistakes?

I believe that a good part of what makes parents wonderful is that they are well-suited to parenting their particular child or children, and that their parenting also fits the times in which they live. Similarly, I think that poor parenting does not fit either the parent or the child; "awful" parenting generally is really inattentive to the needs of the children, or very inconsistent, unpredictable, and hard for the children to understand. If your parents' approach to parenting worked for them and it worked well for you, that's great. If your parents were neglectful or abusive, that's a big burden to shoulder. But you are now a parent yourself, and you get to decide how to do that. Each family has unique personalities, other family members, neighborhood influences, finances, community attitudes, and current social norms to consider; your parents' parenting techniques, good or bad, may not be applicable to *your* parenting situation.

Judith, the child of a single mom, felt that her mother was never available when she was a child, and she vowed that she would be the kind of mother who volunteered at school, brought home-baked snacks to Brownie meetings, and was active in every aspect of her children's lives. Once she had children, though, she felt overwhelmed and uncomfortable with the goals she had set for herself. She found she hated baking and couldn't sustain interest in playing with her children for hours. She missed her job and she liked her home to be especially clean and tidy. Her expectations of herself as a mother were not in keeping with who she really was as a person. She was constantly disappointed in herself and in her children, so even though she tried to do what she felt was right, her kids felt her disappointment and frustration, and her trying to be an ever-present stay-at-home mom failed miserably. Her efforts to "correct" her own parenting didn't work because they didn't take into consideration who she and her children were as specific people.

People are all different. Some moms adjust easily and thrive on being the all-giving earth mother while others feel trapped. Some children adore having mom in the classroom, or as the scout leader, while others prefer that their childhood experiences be separate from their mother's. We all know that some children respond well to firm, clear expectations while others require more discussion and explanations before they are willing to comply. Parents are also comfortable with different styles of parenting, and trying to be a different kind of parent than you are meant to be may be very awkward or unsuccessful.

As difficult as this is to do, great parenting comes from parents who know who they are as individuals, and they tailor their parenting to fit the needs of their current family. They know their own strengths and weaknesses, their children's needs, abilities, and quirks, and accept them all. They also know when to get help, when to be active, when to hold back. They generally do not parent according to some textbook or expert, but according to general parenting principles, like being honest, consistent, reliable, and fair, and with the attitudes and aptitudes of their children as well as themselves in mind. They love the children that they have, even if they aren't who or what they might have chosen, and they accept themselves enough to be real, to listen to the kids, and to tailor their parenting strategies to fit everyone's ages, personalities, and needs.

The idea here is not to be the parent you had or wished you'd had, but to be the parent that your kids need, to the best of your ability given the kind of person you are. If you know you have a problem with patience, work on it. If you know that you can't stand nursery rhymes and your toddler loves them, get someone else to read to him. Provide for your children's needs while being honest about who you are as a person, and you will be a great parent.

I feel terrible, but I yell at my kids way too much. How can I stop that?

You're off to a good start if you are asking this question, because your concern indicates that you don't feel good about having to yell to get your point across to your children. Some families are perfect-ly comfortable with great amounts of yelling and screaming; the kids and parents all know that they are loved and respected, despite the high decibel level. If the yelling doesn't seem too angry and mean to your kids, and you all feel safe and well loved, this really isn't much of a problem. But if the yelling makes you or your kids uncomfortable, or if you feel the raised voices in your house reflect a problem in communication and respect, you are right to be con-cerned, and to attempt to lower the volume.

Once you routinely resort to yelling at your kids, when yelling is the only way you seem able to get a point across, everyone becomes immune to it. Yelling and screaming become the typical means of communication, and that's generally not too pleasant. Your home becomes a place filled with angry and ineffective orders and requests, and your children come to believe that you don't mean what you say unless you are furious and bellowing.

When children believe that unless Mom is screaming, they need not take her seriously, they learn not to listen to her until she raises her voice. You don't really want your children to learn that people don't mean what they say unless they're really irate, nor do you want to live in an atmosphere in which you must be annoyed, or worse, and display your anger verbally before you are heard. But if you are yelling too much of the time, that's what you've got.

It may take some effort to change this pattern. Sometimes it helps to figure out how all this yelling started in the first place. Some parents try so hard to make the children feel valued and respected that they don't teach the children to respect and value *them*. They seem almost afraid to assert any authority over their children. Instead of setting clear expectations and age-appropriate chores for each family member, they coddle the children, do everything for them, and then seem surprised when the children don't respond respectfully or are unwilling to do even the minimum of chores.

When Molly, who has become quite the yeller, politely asks her eight-year-old daughter, Jenny, to pick her clothes up off the floor of her room, Jenny ignores her. When Jenny doesn't reply or respond, Molly counters by raising her voice and repeating the command. She continues to raise her voice until she is finally shrieking at Jenny. Since Molly is afraid to lay down the rules to Jenny, calmly and clearly, that her clothes must be picked up before they go to ballet class, Jenny will never learn that she needs to listen to Molly, and Molly will continue to have to resort to yelling.

If instead, Molly simply asks her nicely first, in a regular voice, and then makes it clear to Jenny (also calmly and quietly) that they won't leave for her class unless the clothes have been picked up, Jenny will start listening to her mother long before Molly's voice is strained. Of course, Molly has to stick to her guns and refuse (still calmly) to take Jenny until the chore has been done. If she can do this, Jenny will learn to listen to her mom, and Molly will eliminate the need for yelling.

It's very difficult to change a pattern to which everyone has become accustomed. The following hints may help you out:

- You might start out by explaining that you don't want to yell anymore, and that you expect your children to start listening to you the first time you make a request.
- Make it clear that you will not raise your voice to get their attention, but there will be consequences if they do not listen.
- Whenever you try to talk with them, make sure you have their attention before asking them to do a chore or finish their homework. Turn off the radio or television before

talking to your kids. Allow them to get off the phone or turn off the Internet so that you know you have their attention. Then talk to them.

- ❀ If your kids yell at you, do not escalate the interaction by yelling back. In a calm voice, tell them that you will listen to them only when they can speak to you in a normal conversational tone. Do not respond to them unless they speak to you calmly, even if that means waiting several minutes—or more.

- ❀ Apologize if you forget to use a calm tone yourself. Work together to make this change, and help each other recognize when your voices start to get out of control.

- ❀ Assess your ability to handle anger and frustration. Figure out if you are yelling because you are frustrated by your children, in which case you need to change the way you all interact, or if you are actually angry about something unrelated to motherhood, like maybe an unsatisfying marriage or job. If you are upset in another area of your life, face what is bothering you so that you can solve the real problem, and don't take it out on the wrong people.

You and your children deserve to be treated with respect. You all need to be heard and to know that you are safe, emotionally as well as physically. Although some families do manage to be pretty comfortable with a lot of yelling, most agree that they prefer it when they listen to each other carefully, help each other out when asked, and in general, treat each other with love and respect. Most of the time, if the mom feels there is too much yelling, solving the underlying causes of the yelling not only decreases the unpleasant interactions among family members; it also improves all their relationships.

I've forgotten to pick up my child at preschool! (Or I'm always the last one to get my child.) I feel like I've scarred her for life.

As strange as this may seem, I know many moms and dads who have forgotten to pick up a child at one time. This feels terrible to everyone involved, no doubt, but unless this is a chronic problem, you needn't worry about permanent psychic scarring. What you might need to figure out is if this is a one-time mental collapse or a constant issue so that you solve the problem rather than simply worry about its impact on your child.

Being late to pick your child up, or forgetting him or her, happens occasionally to nearly all parents. If it is a rare occurrence, simply explain to your child what happened, even if you were just confused about what day it was. Don't focus too much on your own guilt about it; attend to your child's emotions. Your goal is to make your child feel better, not wallow in your own guilt, make yourself feel better, or inadvertently make him or her feel bad that you are so upset. Make sure your little one knows that you would *never* forget her on purpose, and assure her that you will do everything to avoid this problem in the future. Listen to her concerns, and reassure her that she was safe and that the adults who were with her would always take care of her until you arrive.

If this is the only time you've ever forgotten to pick up your child, there is probably nothing much you need to worry about in the long term. Most of the moms I know who have made similar mistakes were overworked or dealing with some kind of unusual situation on that day. Some have come to realize that when the school schedule changes, they are thrown off; they make plans, thinking that their child will be in school until the usual time of 11:30, when on the Day of Forgetfulness, the kids were ready to go home at 11:00. These kinds of mistakes can usually be prevented from reoccurring if the mom keeps a detailed and frequently updated calendar, noting her child's school schedule for every day and making changes in her plans whenever necessary. What's important here is to check that calendar daily so that you are reminded that Wednesdays are always earlier dismissal, for example, or that this coming Thursday there are teacher conferences and no school at all.

If the problem is more chronic, you must make some adjustments. If you are *always* late to get your kids from school, you need to plan ahead and get off to an earlier start. If you can't head to school sooner because of inflexible commitments, you may do well to hire someone or work out a carpool schedule so that you or someone you trust will always be able to meet your kids on time.

If you *could* get to school earlier, but just get engrossed in an activity or become oblivious to the passing of time, using an alarm clock or other electronic reminder could help you get to your child on time.

- Plan to leave your home or job at least several minutes ahead of your usual time, particularly if you have another child to bring along.
- Keep ahead of schedule by remembering that extra time is required when you must also dress and buckle a younger child into a car seat or put your papers away before leaving.
- Don't schedule meetings for right before you must leave.
- Ignore the phone ringing as you walk out the door; this is why answering machines were invented.
- Remember that being on time means a lot to little ones (and to preschool teachers or other child-care folks) and figure out what stops you from picking up your kids on time.
- Change your routine or do whatever it takes to help you arrive more promptly.

If you are chronically late or forgetful, this could be more serious. You may be overcommitted and need more support to meet all your responsibilities. You may have sleep deprivation or some underlying psychological or medical issue that could cause you to be mentally unfocused. Find out what is causing your inability to pick up your child on time. You owe it to yourself to discover if you have problems that prevent you from being the kind of mom you want to be, and you owe it to your children to be able to be reliable and trustworthy. Your children won't be permanently damaged as long as you address the issue head on, solve the problem if it is chronic, and reassure them that you love them and will always do your best to be there for them.

I inadvertently caused an accident which left my child with a scar. He's absolutely fine, but how can I get over the guilt?

Parents often feel worse than their kids do if their kids are hurt, even when it's clearly by mistake or accident, and if they feel they have caused the hurt, parents can be devastated. Jamie, a new mother, was feeding her son, Sam, in a high chair when the boy wriggled his way free of the seat belt, stood up, and promptly fell on his head. He fussed and cried for awhile, but poor Jamie was convinced that Sam was permanently damaged, and that it was all her fault. She called her husband, who rushed home from work only to find Sam playing happily and Jamie in tears.

Sometimes children get hurt no matter how hard we try to protect them. Accidents happen to even the most careful people. When something bad happens, you must deal with it, but once the danger passes, you must be able to move beyond it. Your guilt, while understandable, has no value. Unless you were truly neglectful before, guilt won't make you a better parent and it certainly won't help your child. In fact, guilt can be damaging because it influences you to be either too cautious or too indulgent.

Please forgive yourself. You and your children have long lives ahead of you, and no matter how hard you try to prevent them, there may be other problems and injuries from which you will not be able to protect your kids. Beating yourself up over an accident, even a devastating accident, won't undo whatever damage was done, and it may render you unable to handle the responsibilities and emotions that follow. Forgiving yourself allows you to have a positive relationship with your children and shows them an excellent example of how to manage in difficult situations. We all make mistakes, and you and your children must learn to handle the issues, adjust to the problems, and forgive yourselves and each other.

Most of the time, the child heals faster than the mother who feels she's at fault. It's natural to feel bad for awhile, but try to move beyond it. If your child has any continuing problems as a result of an accident you inadvertently caused, he will need your full commitment, competence, and love. If he's fine, he needs you to return to your regular, relaxed, and comfortable self. Your guilt will do none of you any good. You and your whole family need you to be able to function fully and confidently, and guilt gets in the way. If you can't accept what happened, if you can't forgive yourself, then seek professional help. Everybody makes mistakes, and accidents happen. Forgive yourself, let go of the guilt, and get help if you can't.

Am I a bad mother if sometimes I'm so tired I don't wake up immediately when one of my children calls out to me in the middle of the night?

You are not a bad mother! Your ability to sleep when a child is calling out to you says that you sleep very soundly; it does not reflect how good or bad you are as a mom. Many good moms and dads sleep though their children's night noises, and many not-so-good moms and dads wake easily. The soundness of your sleep is simply that and nothing else.

What's more bothersome than sleeping through your children's requests for nighttime attention is that your expectations of yourself might be too high. We seem to have unreasonable ideas about what it means to be a good parent, and somehow we believe that every whimper from the next room should rouse us to action. While many parents do actually seem to sleep lighter when their children are young, tuned in to every peep coming nightly from their children's rooms, it's okay if you're able to sleep through those snuffles and sleep noises. In fact, there may be benefits to you and your children because your ignoring minor sounds or cries of discomfort may help the kids learn to soothe themselves back to sleep, and you will awake more well-rested.

When children are very young, it can ease a mother's mind to have her little one sleep in the same room with her. The "family bed" has great appeal to many families because the baby is snuggled into bed with the parents, allowing mom or dad to comfort or feed the baby with minimal disturbance to their sleep. Many moms nurse their babies in bed and both drift back to sleep in the process. Proponents of the family bed appreciate the ease and intimacy it provides family members. Everybody feels warm and cozy, and often, parents get a little extra well-deserved rest.

Although the family bed continues to gain acceptance in this country (and, indeed, is the norm in many other countries and cultures), there are also those who believe it is not a particularly safe practice. Opponents worry that babies might be smothered by bedding or if a deeply sleeping parent rolls over on them. An additional concern is that the baby will have difficulty making the transition to sleeping alone, which can be hard on both parents and baby. The family bed seems to work well for families when the parents don't mind helping the baby make a comfortable switch to sleeping alone when he gets a bit older.

There are now special beds specifically designed for babies to sleep safely alongside the parent's bed. This way the baby doesn't actually sleep in the same bed as the parents, eliminating the fear of smothering or squishing the baby while you sleep. It also encourages the baby to be comfortable sleeping alone, but the baby is close and easily heard. As long as the baby is very young, this might help you feel more confident that you will be able to wake up and take care of your tiny one.

If you have a very young or medically compromised child sleeping in another room, though, and you want to be able to wake when they call out to you, you may do well to invest in a baby monitor. I know families that also use these for even older children because the monitor allows the parents to hear what is going on in the child's room and assess whether or not they are needed immediately. If you sleep so soundly that even a shrill and desperate cry won't rouse you, a monitor may ease your mind. With a sleep monitor placed near your ear, you can still sleep soundly, knowing that any serious cry for help will be heard.

Please don't attribute to yourself some dark, nefarious parenting deficit simply because you are a very deep and probably very tired sleeper. Teach your children to come and get you when they truly need you and invest in a baby monitor so you can hear your premobile children's cries for help. Don't waste your energy feeling guilty about a trait over which you have little control and is in no way the sign of bad mothering.

I was really angry the other day and screamed at my child that he was an idiot. Was that as bad as I think it was?

Most parents have probably done something just as unpleasant to their children at one time or another, though they don't generally like to admit it. Fortunately, one incident will not ruin an otherwise positive and warm connection; your relationship with your children develops, grows, and changes over time, and it is the wholeness of your relationship, not just one lapse of self-control on your part, that really matters. While your kids may remember you losing your temper and calling them names as being very upsetting, you have time on your side. If you want to be a better parent, you can; if you have always been a better parent until this episode, you will continue to be.

There are lots of parenting books available, and many are pretty clear about what you should or shouldn't do. Probably no expert would recommend that you call your child an idiot, but it's quite likely that you and your child can both get over this. Talk with your child about what happened and apologize. Explain why you became so angry that you lost self-control. Help her understand that even adults lose their tempers and say things that they don't mean. Often, although they know better, people become so angry that they temporarily are unable to exercise good judgment. Make sure that your child knows that you know you said something that you sincerely regret.

And admit that you made a terrible mistake. Ideally, this should be done almost immediately after the incident, as soon as your head is clear enough to address your inappropriate name calling without getting involved in the issue that led to the outburst. While it is okay to mention that you were particularly angry because your child repeatedly ignored your requests for him to stop playing catch in the living room, ultimately breaking your great-grandmother's favorite vase, do not get immersed in the initial problem or try to blame your child's misbehavior for yours. While your anger may have been justifiable, you both need to understand that name-calling is not acceptable. Apologize for hurting his feelings, assure him that you don't think that he is an idiot at all, and promise that you'll work on never calling him names again.

Although I truly believe that apologizing for hurting your child is important, please do not take my comments to mean that if you apologize, you can continue to do or say hurtful things to your children. Having an adult apologize is a powerful experience if it happens only rarely, and an apology is particularly valuable when it's followed by a change in the parent's troublesome behavior. Relying on apologies, though, to mend a repeatedly damaged relationship won't work. If saying you're sorry isn't sincere, or if the hurtful behavior continues, the child will feel the emptiness behind the apology, and the hurt you inflict on the child will be compounded by resentment.

If you handle this properly, you and your child can learn important lessons. You each learn that even adults make mistakes. You can explore with your child the difference between being angry, which may be appropriate on occasion, and being mean or hurtful, which is not acceptable. You can learn to accept that love and anger aren't mutually exclusive; you can be angry with someone that you love very much. You can begin to understand that there are many ways to express anger, and that some are more effective, appropriate, and grown up than others. You can learn to help each other handle anger appropriately, to discuss the behaviors that infuriate, and to respond to difficult situations with loving firmness. You can learn to be forgiving and to accept forgiveness.

Speaking of forgiveness, not only should you and your children learn to forgive the mistakes of others, you must learn to forgive yourself. You made a mistake. Learn from it and move on. Do not dwell on it, as your child will sense that mistakes are intolerable, or perhaps play on your guilt to get you to be more lenient or indulgent than reasonable. Show by your behavior in the future that you can manage your anger productively, that you can deal with your child's misbehavior in a constructive way. Learn to sense when your anger is bubbling out of control; walk away from a potentially volatile situation so that you can face the problem later, when you have a clearer mind.

Forgive yourself, and learn from your mistakes. Just because you are the mom doesn't mean that you have all the answers, never make a mistake, and never lose your temper. Certainly, try your best not to allow yourself to lose control like this again, but know that the repair work you do in this situation can be the kind of parent–child interchange that can lead to greater maturity if handled well.

My older daughter's life is filled with classes and activities. Is it cruel that I keep dragging my younger daughter along?

People have different attitudes about this question. I know several moms who hire a baby-sitter so as to avoid making the younger child tag along, others who can't spend the money for a sitter, and still others who believe that when siblings tag along, they learn something from observing, and that they are supporting each other's interests and activities. I don't think there is a one-size-fits-all answer to this question.

Part of living in a family is that we do our best to support each others' interests and talents, and that includes even the youngest kids. Of course, a wiggly toddler can't be expected to sit in a car seat for hours every afternoon, but if you are driving short distances and can let your child out to release some of that energy between drives, I don't see why it isn't okay to have her come with you. Besides, make it clear that when she is ready to take classes and go to her own activities, you will make sure she has plenty of opportunities to pursue her interests, too.

If there is a significant age and activity gap, you might want to consider ways to make carpooling and waiting for the older child more fun. Try what Linda did. Her youngest is seven years younger than her oldest child, and as a result, spent a lot of time driving to and from the first child's music lessons and waiting for them to be over. But Linda was very clever; lesson time became the time reserved for Linda and her youngest to play games together, go on walks, or sometimes go for a treat. Instead of dreading his sister's drum lessons, Linda and her youngest looked forward to their weekly checkers game. With a little creativity, class time for the older children can turn into special time for your younger child, too.

I also know several families that have chosen to hire sitters instead. Particularly when both kids have lots of lessons and homework, some parents believe that their children's time can be better spent at home with a sitter than in the backseat of a car going from lesson to lesson. If money isn't an issue, I see no problem hiring a sitter to play with the younger child while you take the older child, or, if you hire a sitter who can drive, having the sitter drive the older child while you stay at home and help the younger ones with homework or bake cookies together.

I also know moms who arrange for lessons and classes to be on weekends or later in the evenings when dad is available to help out. Still others make play dates for the younger kids at the same time as the class or lesson. While Mom and the older child are attending the class or practice, the younger child is visiting a friend's house. You just need to make sure you reciprocate with regular dates at your own home, ideally at times that help the other mom, so that the arrangement is beneficial to everyone.

You have to know your own kids, your family's needs, and your financial limits. When after-school activities can provide an opportunity for playing with the younger child, you won't feel that you're dragging her along; you'll feel that you're having some really great and memorable times together. But if having the other child along always seems a struggle, scheduling classes when dad is around, hiring a sitter, or finding a compatible playmate with an agreeable mom makes more sense. Do what works for your family, your kids, and your budget, and don't feel bad about whatever choice makes sense for you.

I nag my children and my husband. We all hate my nagging, but how else can I get them to do what I want them to do?

Does nagging even work? Probably not. If you all hate your nagging, and it doesn't work very well anyway, it's time to figure out what started you nagging in the first place and what you can do instead.

So ask yourself, why do you nag? And why doesn't your family respond to you without nagging? You ask your daughter nicely to make her bed, and she ignores you. You ask again, a little less nicely, and she tells you she'll do it later. You wait a bit, then ask her again, a little sharper, and she snaps back, "I *told* you I'd do it later!" By now, you are both aggravated. She tells you to stop nagging, you yell at her to make the bed; this simple request has turned ugly and the bed is still unmade. Nagging doesn't seem to get family members to be more responsive or obedient, and it might actually be counterproductive. Since everyone knows that Mom isn't really serious until she's nagged you repeatedly, why bother to react if she hasn't gotten really worked up yet?

Instead of nagging, ask once for what you want or expect. Determine the consequences for noncompliance, make them appropriate and clear, and then follow through. Next time you ask your daughter to make her bed, give her a specific time it must be done. Ask her to make it before she comes to breakfast, if that's the family rule. Then tell her, nicely and calmly, that the new rule is, no breakfast until her bed is made. *Then stick by the rule.*

Do not get upset (and certainly don't cave in and make her a meal) if she doesn't eat because she continues not to make her bed. She may miss breakfast for a couple of days, but you will have stopped nagging. If she demands that you get her some toast, you peacefully reply that the toast will be ready after she's made her bed. If she tries to engage you in an argument, you must politely and evenly respond that she knew that the rule is no breakfast until the bed is made. Pretty soon, if she wants breakfast, the bed will get made.

Make rules that make sense (for example, don't withhold breakfast if your child never eats breakfast or prepares it for herself) and do not change the rules without telling your family first. Whenever possible, allow enough time for others to finish what they are doing before tackling what you want from them; don't expect them to drop everything to do what you ask immediately, but do expect them to do what you've asked in a reasonable amount of time. Tell your family that you are no longer going to nag and that their cooperation will help. Then just stop nagging.

Recognize that some mothers nag not because their family members ignore them but because they want more control in their lives. Theresa hated the fact that nine-year-old Andrew wouldn't do his homework right after school, when she thought he should, so she nagged and nagged every afternoon. He would stall, eating a snack, turning on the TV, calling a friend, playing with the dog, until he felt ready to return to his books about an hour later. Finally, he pointed out to his mom that he was getting great grades, even though he never started his homework until later in the day. She realized that he needed do some things his way, and that his way was just as good as hers. Theresa stopped nagging, at least about homework.

Make sure what you are requesting makes sense, and that there are logical and reasonable consequences when others don't do what you've asked of them. Then, if you catch yourself nagging again anyway, take a deep breath and walk away. Although it can be hard to break bad habits, you can do it! Maintain a quiet demeanor and think about your goal. If you want others to do what's best for them, then respect the fact that they might know as well as you do what that really means. If you feel that they just don't help or respect you, then stop nagging, take the calmer approach suggested above, and your composed behavior, combined with clear and natural consequences for not being more helpful, should make a big difference.

Sometimes my kids will ask for something really frivolous, and I'll say "no" almost without thinking. How can I decide when indulging a silly request might be appropriate versus when it would lead to spoiling the child?

Some parents seem to say "no" to everything while others seem to say "yes" to everything, and neither is probably in the best interests of the children. When trying to decide when to say yes and no, you should consider your financial situation and the difference between *need* and *want*. You also need to be clear about your family values, including what sorts of things you want your children to work for and what you believe should be treats.

Your finances must be considered. Although this seems obvious, you should not buy things you cannot afford. If you sacrifice buying nutritious groceries in order to buy $200 name-brand athletic shoes for a seven-year-old, you may be indulging the child's wishes to have shoes all his classmates will envy, but you are also teaching him that looking good is more important than eating well. If what your child wants will cause your family to be unable to pay essential bills, then it's appropriate to say "no," or at least to say, "We can't afford that right now, but let's save up to buy that for you." This way, you don't buy what you can't pay for, and you're not simply denying your child's request. You're being honest about what your family can afford, teaching your child that money must sometimes be budgeted, and helping him learn that it's worth it to wait for something he truly wants.

If money is not an object, then making these decisions is a bit trickier. You don't want to give your children absolutely everything they ever ask for because they will not learn to value work or the things themselves. Then you need to think about how to be loving and generous without being overindulgent. Helping your child understand the difference between wanting something and needing it is a good place to begin.

To me, something is frivolous if you truly don't *need* it, or, as in the example of the costly athletic shoes, if it is an unnecessarily higher priced version of a necessity. You may *want* the designer version, but what you *need* are shoes, and the discount department store brand would be just fine. As parents, you must decide how much you value style over cost, on what items, and when to go ahead and be frivolous.

And I highly encourage occasional frivolity. It feels great to indulge a beloved child, and the child enjoys being indulged. With a surprise treat, or an unexpected "yes," you and your child can be lighthearted and easy together, and that's lovely. What's fun about that frivolous indulgence is the unexpected and unusual aspect of it.

Frivolous indulgence spills over into spoiling, though, when the child believes that he should or will always get whatever he wants. When a child believes that all he needs to do is ask and he will receive, he doesn't learn the value of money, how to work for what he wants, how to budget, or how to make thoughtful choices. He feels entitled to things without making any effort. When you constantly say "yes," indulgence loses its charm; it becomes an expectation and entitlement.

If you *always* say "no," though, pretty soon children will stop asking, and they will feel that you are stingy, extremely poor, don't care about their perceived needs and desires, or that you feel that they don't deserve anything. You don't want to burden children with your financial woes, or make them believe that you don't consider their needs or wants.

If you can't afford to indulge a request, be matter-of-fact about it, and suggest an alternative. Treats don't need to be expensive nor do they need to be frequent to help your child feel that they are valued and loved. Taking your kids to the park for half an hour instead of making them start their homework right after school can be a wonderful treat. Making cookies at home can satisfy the desire for store-bought. The point is, being thoughtful about how and when you say "no" will work better for you and your family.

Strive for a comfortable middle ground. Give to your child when you can and when it feels like what you are giving will be enjoyed and appreciated. Say "no" when the request is clearly unreasonable or you cannot afford it. Try to make these decisions based on the needs of the child, both emotionally and practically, as well as on your financial ability to give in to these requests. Consider each request seriously and individually. If you indulge your children when time, money, and circumstances permit, neither spoiling nor feelings of deprivation should be a problem.

My children already have a lot of homework. Am I supposed to help or should I let them do it on their own, even if I know I could help them do better?

Of course you could help them do it better; chances are you already passed third grade. The real question here is when to help and when not to help. And the key word is *help*.

My policy is that homework is the child's responsibility; the parent's responsibility is to see that the child has the time, equipment, environment, support, and encouragement to do the homework. Your children each need a place that is quiet, calm, well-lit, and comfortable to spread out and settle down to do their work, unless they are teenagers, in which case they need music, a phone, and maybe not so much light. Keeping in mind the particular needs of your children, once you've provided them with the necessities, unless they ask you specific questions, that's all the help you need give.

Some kids like to do their homework alone in their rooms while others want to be near Mom, and either way is fine. Some kids truly need help, and that is also fine. If they are having trouble interpreting an assignment, they need you to get them four sheets of orange poster board, or they'd like you to drill them on their science facts, your support can be invaluable. When they have trouble in a particular subject and you can spend some extra time with them to make sure they really understand the concept, that's wonderful. But when your fifth grader is supposed to make a model of an igloo out of sugar cubes, it's sometimes hard to know when to stop helping.

But stop you must. Unless you plan to follow your child around for the rest of his life doing his work for him, he must learn to meet his responsibilities himself. If he can't do an assignment, and you can't help him learn the material, he needs to let his teacher know that. When you step in and do your child's work without helping him learn the material himself, it shakes his self-confidence and limits his learning. Doing too much of his work for him makes him feel either that his work isn't good enough for you, or that when he can't or doesn't feel like working, you will step in and make sure he gets a good grade whether or not he learns the concepts. Those are not good lessons.

Help your child understand an assignment, study for a test, organize his time and materials, or grapple with a difficult concept until he truly comprehends it. Help him proofread his work by pointing out and explaining his errors; don't correct them yourself. Help him to become a confident student by offering loving support and encouraging him to do his work himself. If he can't keep up with his assignments, arrange a meeting with him and his teacher; a child should be able to do his homework fairly well in a reasonable amount of time without undue help on your part, and if he can't, he may need extra support or tutoring. That's okay! That may be who your child is! Helping him by doing his work for him undermines his confidence if he is a capable student and masks potential learning problems if he is struggling. His teacher needs to know if he feels overwhelmed or unable to handle his homework, or if he is overly dependent on your involvement, because it is her job to make sure your child is learning appropriately.

If he manages his homework just fine without you, relax and help only when asked. If the homework seems consistently to be beyond his ability, you can help him best by consulting with his teacher so that she understands how he is really doing and offers the guidance he needs. Support your child's efforts to be an independent, diligent, and thoughtful student. That's what will be truly helpful to him.

I have kids a few years apart, and what works with one doesn't always work with the other. How can I make discipline and rules that seem fair to all?

On the surface, this seems very tricky. One child in the family responds well to a lot of freedom, while the other needs stricter rules and limits. It might seem very unfair to the one who does just fine without rigid rules to have to be home by a specific time, or to call in every couple of hours, and it would be equally foolish to have no family rules or guidelines when one child seems to crave more active and clear limits. What is fair is that you plan your parenting to suit the needs of all your children, even if that means slightly different expectations of each child.

When you're dealing with different kinds of kids, I think guidelines work better than specific rules. For example, if one of your children is a night owl and needs very little sleep relative to your other children, forcing her to be in bed by 8:30 on school nights will frustrate her to no end and not result in a peaceful evening. But if you have other children who truly need a structured and predictable bedtime and routine, having an unenforced bedtime might be problematic for them. Compromise works well here. Bedtime doesn't have to mean sleep time. The family ritual could be that the children will be in their rooms every school night by 8:30 (or whatever times seem appropriate according to the children's ages), and that they may choose whether to go to bed, read, do puzzles, or rest quietly until they are ready to sleep—as long as they are quiet and don't disturb anyone else.

Some children respond well to discussions about everybody's needs being different, and if yours do, then talking about why your expectations may be different for each child may solve your dilemma. Children want what's fair as well as what's appropriate. Explain why you try to tailor your parenting to each child; reassure each one that you are doing your best to provide what each of them wants and needs. Elisa tells her kids that she would no sooner punish each child the same way than she would reward them similarly. Ethan, her older son, is deathly allergic to chocolate, while chocolate is younger son Daniel's favorite sweet. When she wants to treat Ethan, then, she might get him a toy or take him to a movie, but Daniel would much prefer a giant chocolate bar. When they see how appropriate it is to be treated uniquely in a positive way, they understand that what's best for one isn't always best for the other. Use this clever mom's logic to help your children understand why you handle each child individually.

It's perfectly fine and fair to treat your children as unique individuals. As long as your expectations of each child are appropriate to their personalities and levels of development and don't actually favor one over the other, your children should accept and appreciate your treating them as specific and separate people. Adjusting your rules or guidelines as your children grow and develop and keeping them separate but equal can be challenging, but being that responsive to the particular needs of each child will benefit them in the end. Be clear about what you are expecting from each and why, listen to your children's feelings about the family expectations so that everyone feels treated fairly, and the children should have no trouble with your handling issues on a case-by-case basis. In general, they will actually appreciate your wanting to know them and respond to them so fittingly.

With two children, my husband and I seem to have a "divide and conquer" approach to parenting. Is it a bad idea that we seem to split up, one child with each of us, and relatively little time when all of us are together?

I believe that most things, when done in moderation, are just fine, and in excess, well, are excessive, and usually not so fine. If your family members always split up, you are not getting to spend much time as a couple or as a family, and your children will not learn from family living to share, take turns, be patient, or to play together. Many families do use the divide and conquer approach, but I always wonder what they are dividing, and what they need to conquer.

Occasionally splitting up the family is a wonderful approach, particularly when you alternate which child goes with whom. Each child then gets time alone with each parent, and clearly this eliminates the need for compromise or waiting. Each child's interests and abilities are more easily met when there are only one's needs to consider. Splitting the kids between the parents avoids problems developing because the children have different attention spans, skills, or interests. When time alone with a parent is occasional—even when it is the family routine that Dad reads to each child individually every night while Mom bathes the other child and then they switch—it can be very special.

If the kids are almost never together, though, some valuable lessons in family living are lost. When families do things together, children learn to appreciate the tastes and talents of their siblings. It can be a very positive and bonding experience for the older one to join in on an activity chosen by the younger one. I think it is also important for children to attend their sibling's big events. Little sisters and brothers want an audience just as much as their bigger siblings do, yet often, because it seems easier, parents allow older children to stay home, or don't bring littler kids along, leaving them with the other parent. When the whole family attends recitals and games, both older and younger children then feel respected and honored, and neither parent has to miss the special program.

Splitting the family also avoids the issue of teaching your children to be respectful and behaving appropriately in a variety of situations. I think having children learn "museum manners" or "restaurant behavior" from an early age enriches them as individuals and offers them opportunities for growth that participating in only activities of their own choosing can't. Obviously, I'm not advocating taking your infant and two-year-old to a

Wagnerian opera, but I believe that children thrive when exposed to a variety of experiences and are expected to behave themselves appropriately. It won't always work, and there will almost certainly be times when one parent will be forced to remove a child whose patience had evaporated. But doing things as a family, expecting children to be respectful of each other's interests, and being supportive audience members or spectators at sibling's activities increases patience, may broaden interests, and builds memories that children can share forever.

So divide and conquer when you want some focused time for each child, and do things as a family whenever possible. Forge strong ties between your children by having family outings, attending each family member's important events, and taking turns choosing fun things to do. Let your children play together and occasionally squabble, as that helps them learn how to get along, how to compromise, and how to take turns. Don't separate them unnecessarily; use the divide and conquer method as just one method in an arsenal of good parenting techniques and you and your children will be fine.

Mealtimes are a disaster at my house; the kids refuse to eat anything but peanut butter and jelly, and we are constantly battling with them about table manners. What should we do?

Family mealtimes may be the only time of the day when the entire family gathers, so you want that time to be pleasant, not something that everybody dreads. I know several families who have turned what should be a lovely daily experience into one that no one looks forward to anymore. Choose your battles. If you want your family dinners to be enjoyable, don't use that time to bring up a poor test score or to criticize your daughter's posture, because then mealtimes will become a time of tension. Although demanding a certain level of civility at mealtimes is reasonable, remember that your goal is to enjoy each other's company and create a warm and loving environment. Mealtime should be pleasurable, not painful.

Here's what I think are some realistic and manageable ideas to make mealtimes together more pleasant for everyone. Keep rules simple, straightforward, and manageable by and applicable to all family members.

- The most essential element in mealtime etiquette for a loving family should be that each family member will be treated with respect and fondness at each meal. That means that there is no name-calling, taunting, or harsh criticism, and everyone's opinions are equally valued. Each family member should be encouraged to share news of his or her day and to listen to the comments of all others.

- One rule might be that eating does not begin until everyone is served. This is generally considered to be good manners, it encourages all diners to be prompt, and it is respectful of whoever is responsible for getting the food onto the table. Everybody eating at the same time facilitates conversation and a more relaxed pace.

- Except on rare occasions, do not watch television while eating dinner. It might be okay during the State of the Union Address or the Super Bowl, but if you are watching TV, you are not interacting with each other. Watch TV when you watch TV; eat dinner together and visit with each other when it's mealtime.

- Basic table manners should be expected. That means chewing with closed mouths, no reading, no feet on the table, and not eating so fast that one diner finishes eating before everyone has a chance to talk with each other.

- When manners fail, a gentle reminder may be offered. Remember to keep your expectations realistic. A two-year-old is likely incapable of feeding him or herself without making a mess. A teenager, however, should be able to chew with his mouth closed and not reach across the table or grab food from another's plate. Do not, however, turn meal time into a battle for control, and do not nag. If a family member has a real problem with table manners, instruct the child lovingly at another time how to hold the knife.

- Model good behavior yourself. Many times I have been amazed to hear parents complain that their children have poor manners, yet they themselves are rude to each other or to the kids. If you politely ask your husband to pass the bread, and then wait patiently for the bread to make it around the table, your children will learn from your behavior. If you get up and leave the table while your child is talking, use unacceptable language, or reach across the table to help yourself to seconds, your children will learn that.

- Don't fight with your kids about what they eat. While it's not what's recommended, many healthy children go through much of their childhoods eating nearly the same foods day after day. Encourage them to try a variety of foods, but don't use food as either a threat or a reward.

- Pushing children to finish their vegetables in order to get some treat emphasizes the reward aspect of sweets, which really isn't such a good idea. Similarly, don't force your child to finish everything on his plate if he is no longer hungry. He will learn not to pay attention to when he is full. Instead, start with much smaller portions so less is wasted.

- If everyone likes different foods, you can accommodate their varied tastes without feeling like you're running a restaurant. In my family, we have one vegetarian and one who eats almost no vegetables. Our meals almost always include something like pasta, potatoes, or rice that everyone likes, cut up fruit or vegetables, and some meat for the carnivores among us. That way I have done my duty, offering starch, meat, and veggies, diners have some choice, and no one leaves hungry.
- Make sure no one dominates the conversation. If you notice that one of you consistently seems to be the biggest talker, turn to the quietest family member and ask, "What do you think?" Everyone should get a turn to talk, and everyone needs to learn to listen.
- Be kind to each other.

Parents who are too strict at mealtimes create miserable memories for their children. Being kind to each other includes eating nicely, listening to each other, taking turns talking, and being respectful of each other's ideas and behaviors. When that's what mealtime is about, the battle is over.

My daughter refuses to wear dresses. I feel like an ogre if I force her, but aren't there times when it is reasonable to demand she wear appropriate attire?

So often in life you have to decide what's really important. Is your daughter a pleasant person? Does she have friends? Does she do okay in school? If you think about all the things she does well, refusing to wear a dress, except when absolutely required by a dress code or the nature of the event, is really not such a big deal.

Many children, boys and girls, prefer to wear one kind of clothing for a while. Some girls hate dresses, some wear only dresses, and some boys refuse to wear anything but T-shirts and jeans. Often the very same girl who wears only skirts or fancy dresses at age five will not touch a skirt or dress when she's a bit older. Some girls eschew the so-called feminine colors when just a couple of years before their closets overflowed with pinks and lavenders.

Most of the time these days, what your child chooses to wear has really very minimal requirements. Your kids must dress appropriately for the situation (a concept which is often loosely defined) and for the weather, and that's it. Color and style are a matter of preference, and even very young children have clear preferences that, within reason, you ought to respect. Your child's choice of clothes reflects his or her personality and is the beginning of him or her becoming a unique individual. That's good, even when that unique individual's taste doesn't coincide with yours, and, within reason, you ought to support that.

Occasionally, there are children who have trouble understanding that their clothing choice is inappropriate or even unhealthy. Some children resist the suggestion that those sandals may not be the best option for a snowy day, and for those kids, experience may be the best teacher. When Lydia was eight years old, she insisted on wearing her favorite sandals to school despite warnings that the sidewalks were covered in snow and slush. Her mom worried that she would arrive at school with cold, wet feet, but Lydia would not budge. Of course, her mother was right, and while Lydia did have some very uncomfortable toes because they became soaked and frozen on her way to and from school, she learned her lesson and never fought about footwear again. Her mom knew that although Lydia would be mighty miserable, she would also be safe because she had to walk a very short way. After advising her otherwise, she allowed Lydia to wear those sandals and thereby learn that sometimes fashion isn't worth the price of serious discomfort.

When proper clothing is essential, as when an all-day hike in the sun requires comfortable shoes and a good hat and sunscreen, or attendance at a formal wedding demands that your daughter finally wear that dress, calmly insist on the requisite outfit. If necessary, make it clear to her that she won't be allowed to attend if she isn't dressed properly. In my experience, though, if you explain why sometimes, for safety or out of respect for a loved one, you must wear things you'd prefer not to, and if you don't insist she wear clothes that she hates most of the time, your daughter will in all probability—although somewhat reluctantly—agree to wear the dreaded dress, snow pants, or the color pink, when necessary.

If your child is allowed to express herself though her clothing, and if she's doing nothing dangerous or immoral, let go of your need to dictate what she wears. A good kid is a good kid, whether she's in shorts or a dress. Show her you respect her, whatever she wears, and when it's important for her to wear something in particular, I'm betting she will.

Our oldest child is a gifted athlete and our youngest is really beautiful. My sister says we're labeling them if we refer to one as the athlete and one as the beauty, but I think it's complimentary. Am I being a bad mom and I don't even know it?

Occasional comments about what each excels at is okay and definitely complimentary, but thinking of Max *only* as an athlete, or of Sophia as just a beauty can have an unintentionally negative impact. While you believe that you are conveying your pride in their skills, accomplishments, or innate gifts, some children perceive those comments differently. Problems may emerge when parents label their kids, even when those labels are completely positive.

When praise is lavished indiscriminately, it loses its value. When praised all the time for what they consider unimpressive efforts or for traits over which they have no control, some children feel that the praise is empty. I've heard children say, "You're my mother; you have to think I'm beautiful." Constant comments about your daughter's beauty or about your son's athletic prowess may be intended to make them feel good, but said too often, and without paying attention to the whole child, can make the child feel that you or they won't even notice when something they do is truly special.

Some children praised solely for their accomplishments wonder if they are loved for their skills or their appearance rather than for who they are as a whole being. Often, very talented kids take little pleasure in their own abilities when they feel that people see them as little more than their abilities. Children certainly want to feel proud about what they do. But if too much attention is paid to the skills or the outcome of the child's actions, and not enough support or enthusiasm is given to the process and thrill of learning new skills, kids begin to believe that it is the accomplishment that is lovable, and not the child him or herself. They even worry that if somehow they lose that skill or beauty, they will no longer be loved.

Labeling also limits some children's ability to recognize their own skills, leading to unfavorable comparisons and competition. Rachael had four children, each one academically gifted. Unfortunately, the third child's intellectual brilliance was in a more creative, less traditionally measurable vein. Although she was arguably as talented as any of the others, she would describe herself as the "dumb" one in the family. Her test scores were in the 97th percentile rather than the 99th, like her siblings. In a less competitive and labeling family, this child would have felt confident in her own intelligence and creativity; labeling the other children as gifted in math or science made her feel she was stupid by comparison.

Labeling within a family can encourage jealousy or competition, limit a child's joy in his accomplishments, or make a child retreat from certain challenges. If a child sees athletics as the sole domain of an older brother, for example, he may never attempt to succeed in sports himself; if Brenna has the role of the smart one, Katrina might not recognize her own intelligence. A positive label for one child may discourage the other children from entering the same activities, or, conversely, encourage children with little innate interest or ability to become involved in something just to please you or to keep up with the revered sibling. Neither is a desired outcome.

Of course, negative labeling is never acceptable, and that is more obvious. A child who is called the fat one, the slow one, or the clumsy one by parents or siblings may suffer from low self-esteem from those labels forever. What's trickier is recognizing that even positive, complimentary labels can be limiting or damaging to children, despite your good intentions. Children want to be appreciated and loved for the people they are, not only for their abilities or deeds.

So try not to label your children even when you believe that the labels are complimentary. Instead, talk to your children about what they enjoy. Discuss why they chose to use so much blue in the painting, rather than simply exclaiming that what they painted is beautiful. Encourage lots of different interests and activities, not just the ones in which your child excels. Love the child for who he is, not for what he does, and show him that love by showing interest in his thoughts, his attitudes, his interests. When you know your child your sincere compliments will show the child that *she* is loved, and admired for the whole person she is, and that is what children really want and need.

Chapter Two

How Mothers Feel

A mother I know loved to sew, so she told her daughter that for her fifth birthday she would make her a special dress. Together they went to a fabric store; the mother and daughter studied the pattern books and examined many bolts of fabric. The daughter chose a pattern and fabric; her fifth birthday dress would have a big white collar with lace, pouffy sleeves, and a big sash, and be made from fabric covered in flowers. The mother worked on the dress for weeks, getting the lace just right, adjusting it to fit, and both mother and daughter looked forward to her wearing it to school for her birthday. On the big day, the little girl received a package from her grandmother and she excitedly tore it open. Inside, she found a beautiful dress, ruffled and frilly, with intricate lacing up the back. She became enchanted with this dress; she wanted to wear that dress to school rather than the dress her mother had made.

The mother was crushed, asking her little girl, "Are you *sure* that's the one you want to wear?" Even at age five, the child could see that her mother was very disappointed, so the daughter answered her mommy, "Yes, but I'll wear the dress you made if you really want me to."

Fortunately, the mother, despite her disappointment, loved and understood her daughter. She appreciated and was moved by her daughter's offer to wear the homemade dress. She also realized that if she asked her daughter to wear the dress she had sewn, she would be acting to fulfill her own needs, not her child's. In the end, the daughter got to wear the fancy dress from Grandma, and the mom was touched by the combination of this little girl's sensitivity to her mother's feelings and her ability to ask for what she wanted.

It is hard work to raise children. Motherhood challenges your heart, your body, your mind, your soul. Most mothers want to be good mothers; they want to give their children all the love, support, guidance, and material goods they need to grow up to become contented, productive, and independent adults. Sometimes it is very clear what children need from their parents, but often, it is not. In addition, I think "experts" tend to focus so much on what the children need from their parents that they don't really take into consideration that the parents are people, too.

Ideally, when a woman becomes a mother, she is reasonably emotionally mature and has a well-defined identity. Ideally, the mother is able to delay her own gratification long enough to take care of the needs of her children, the parents have enough love between them and financial stability to take care of the children's material needs without too much stress, and enough emotional stability to take care of their own emotional needs. In reality, though, parents are people too, and although you may have been extremely well-adjusted and mature when you became a parent, you are still learning about life yourself. You are still growing, developing, thinking about how you fit into the world, working on figuring out your place in life, changing, and learning every day.

I believe that no matter how intelligent, experienced, psychologically mature, or well-adjusted a person is, simply by continuing to live as a conscious human being in this society, he or she is constantly learning, growing, developing, reassessing, and, to a certain extent, reinventing him or herself. I don't think that there is just one period of emotional growth, that one reaches some developmental spot called "adulthood" and then remains emotionally constant or becomes "mature." Every experience in life shapes your attitudes and personality, colors your reactions and the way you see the world, changes how you make decisions and what choices you make. Motherhood is one of those experiences that has an enormous impact on your growth and development.

Somehow we tend to think of mothers, though, as finished products, people who should have the answers and know what they are doing. The parenting experts give excellent advice, but as a parent and a psychotherapist, I know that no one enters motherhood finished with her own development, and, indeed, motherhood continues to shape and alter who that mother is. If that is true, then simply getting advice about what to say or do seems to ignore some important aspects of life as a mother. Advice is great when the recipient of the advice is interested, willing, and able to make use of it, but if the mother's own feelings are too complicated or she has too many unresolved issues, knowing what she should do can become just one more burden and no help to her at all.

Unfortunately, many parenting situations are hard to assess; when each family member wants or needs something different, often at odds with one another, satisfying one person's needs may require that another's go unmet. Figuring out when to take care of which emotions (when one person's emotional needs trump another's) sometimes feels impossible. Even as the mother in the family, your own wishes, your own emotions sometimes get in the way of doing what you know is best.

Parents are just people, too, going about their lives and trying to get through each day. No one really sets about to ruin their children's lives. But sometimes, being a good parent to your children is a lot harder than it appears. Even with the best of intentions, parents act out of their own needs, their own self-interests. Sometimes without thinking, and sometimes due to lack of better understanding, and sometimes just because of the realities of being a person in a complicated world, parents have emotions that they believe they shouldn't. That's what this chapter is all about.

Sometimes, no matter how very much you love your children, you have feelings about them that make you feel guilty. You are disappointed that they favor your husband's side of the family, you wish they were interested in chess instead of comic books, or you get angry about something they did despite knowing that they didn't know any better. Good mothers are still people, people with their own ideas about what their children should be like, people with needs and interests separate from their parenthood, and people who, at the same time they are raising children, are also trying to figure out their own lives.

What might be best for you as an individual might not be best for your family; just when you really want to be able to climb into a cozy chair with a good book, your kids want you to play outside with them. Being a good parent entails juggling many people's needs and desires, and often placing your own wishes last. Delaying your own satisfactions may make you feel virtuous, but it may also make you feel guilty for wanting something for yourself, for not feeling all that magnanimous, or for being annoyed with your kids. No matter how much you want to be a great mother, even if you always try to do the "right" thing, those angry, frustrated feelings may (often unnecessarily or even inappropriately) make you feel guilty.

I have worked with parents, kids, and families for over twenty years, and one thing has become very clear to me; kids get the best parenting when their parents are reasonably well-adjusted, and are specifically well-suited to be the parents of the kind of kids they have. That means that the parents don't have too many of their own emotional issues to get in the way of seeing to the needs of all family members, including themselves, and that they innately understand and respect the specific children they have. Good parents seem automatically to adjust their parenting techniques appropriately to the stage of development and personality of each child. Their own personalities, interests, and energy levels are often compatible with their kids'. Children need parents who love them unconditionally, for being whatever and whoever they are, and who will support their growth and development in ways that meet their individual needs. Sometimes what makes that work most easily is that the kids and the parents are naturally well-matched to each other.

It would seem likely that the parents who feel the least guilt about their parenting are those who never make mistakes, who never feel disappointed by their kids, and who feel anger only rarely. But remember, feeling guilty isn't always about the result of some interaction. It can also be about feeling something that you believe you shouldn't. So mothers often feel guilty when they have emotions toward their children that they deem are unacceptable. I think moms are generally very hard on themselves, and this chapter is intended to give comfort and support to mothers who feel guilty about their emotions, even when they behave well toward their loved ones. Most mothers feel unwelcome emotions at times. While feeling anger or frustration is normal, it is nothing to feel guilty about; feelings and behaviors are two different things, and not everything about motherhood is always rosy.

The questions and answers in this chapter address the many ways in which mothers feel guilty about their feelings and thoughts. This chapter examines what it's like to know you're not as patient as you would like to be, to face the fact that sometimes you just want to get away from everything, that sometimes you don't much like one of your kids. It is about disappointing yourself as well as about how your children may have disappointed you. It provides answers to concerns about how to manage when you feel impatient, judgmental, or angry with your kids. It looks at questions many women have but don't like to acknowledge having about their feelings about motherhood and their feelings about their kids.

Most mothers at least occasionally harbor bad feelings about their kids or about motherhood, and many caring moms feel guilty when they do. Yet it's normal to love your children and be a great mother and still have moments when your feelings aren't all that attractive. The questions and answers in this chapter examine the things moms expect of themselves and help mothers figure out which demands to try to meet, and which are unreasonable or can wait. Mothers don't always understand or accept that their feelings, even when they are unwelcome or uncomfortable, are legitimate and deserve attention. This chapter allows a mother to face her feelings about motherhood.

I want to be a great wife, mother, daughter, worker, and friend. Why is it so hard to do it all?

It is always hard to do a great job at absolutely everything. You probably acknowledge that you have more talents and skills in some areas and less in others, yet you seem to expect yourself to juggle all your social, family, and work roles with expertise and grace, excelling at all of them. You almost certainly do most things very well already. In my experience, the women who ask themselves why it's so hard to be great at everything *are* great at everything. The problem really isn't whether you are good enough or why it is so hard; the problem may be that you haven't set reasonable expectations for yourself, and are trying to be somebody or something that you are not.

Women, and especially mothers, are notoriously tough on themselves. We believe that we are supposed to be totally giving, available to fill the needs of those whom we love, take care of, look up to, and work for, and we expect ourselves to do so easily and well. In most aspects of our lives, once we are involved and committed, we rarely give ourselves the opportunity to examine whether or not we truly value specific relationships, whether we as individuals are actually the best ones to fulfill a particular need, or whether we even want to continue in a particular role. We are not good at sharing or delegating responsibilities. In attempting to do it all gracefully and well, we forget to consider if doing everything really makes sense for us.

We need to pay attention to the demands we place on ourselves and be conscious of how we choose to spend our time and energy. I firmly believe that you can be a great daughter, wife, mother, friend, and worker, but I also believe that women are most successful when they make deliberate and thoughtful choices. That's admittedly hard to do when the demands of home, family, and work seem to collide, but facing the demands and thinking about how you want to meet them will help you feel more successful at all of them.

Take the time, once a week, once a month, once a day, if that works for you, to think about what is important to you. If you really enjoy seeing your coworker, Sarah, make plans to get together with her, but if you get tense and exhausted when you have to deal with your boss's secretary, do what you can to limit that contact. Limit your interactions with people and situations you don't enjoy and make time for those that give you pleasure. Whenever possible, eliminate relationships and chores that feel burdensome. Be willing to delegate the chores you don't manage well to others who do. Tolerate your own limitations, accommodate them, and you will not only be successful at what you do, you will feel more successful.

When your expectations of yourself are more in accordance with your skills and preferences, you will be doing what matters to you. When you are realistic about what you can do and for whom you want to be doing it, you will feel that you are accomplishing more of what you want to be accomplishing. You will be great at what's necessary and important to you, which is really what matters after all. And then you will feel better about how you are managing all the demands and pleasures of your life.

How can I learn to say "no" kindly and appropriately?

"My kids (or my husband or friends) ask me to do things for them and I always seem to say yes, even when what they ask may be inconvenient or unpleasant for me," complained Susan. "Why is it so hard to say 'no'?"

This is a question many mothers ask; women often feel that they need to please others in order to be accepted or loved. However, you are entitled to decide how it is best for you to spend your time and other resources. That means that whether you have plans to take a nap or to go to work, it is acceptable to consider your needs as well as the needs of your friends or relatives.

When you have lots of different relationships and roles, you naturally have many pulls on your time and energy, but that doesn't require you to fill all requests. You have the right and responsibility to yourself and to your family to decide if and when to say "yes," and you also have the right and responsibility to yourself and family to say "no." If you have always been an accommodating and giving person, it will take some practice before you are able to say "no" graciously and without too much discomfort. And keep in mind that, at least at first, the discomfort will be greater for you than for the person you may be turning down.

When asked to do something that makes you feel pressured or overwhelmed, face your feelings. You do no one any favors in the long run if you allow yourself to become a pushover. The people in your life who genuinely love you may want your help or opinion or companionship, but if they love you unconditionally, they do not want anything from you at your expense. If a relationship falls apart because you can't or won't do someone a favor, then that wasn't much of a friendship, was it?

When saying, "yes" to someone makes your stomach churn or your head pound, you must learn to say "no." Chances are if you feel the need to say "no," you have a very good reason. Share your reason if you want to, but keep it simple.

- If there is a clear conflict, just say so. "I can't take care of your baby next Tuesday because I've got plans with my sister."
- Even if you don't have a direct conflict, it's okay to say "no" if you will be too tired or rushed. "I have a doctor's appointment that afternoon, and I just must be able to get my chores done first. So sorry."

- Offer alternative solutions if you have any. "I can't do it on Thursday, but if you can wait, I could help you out on Friday."
- If you don't want to explain why you have to turn someone down, don't. "I'm so sorry, I just won't be able to help you out." You don't owe anyone more information than you are comfortable sharing. On those rare times when someone presses you for an explanation, simply say that you're sorry, but you just can't go into the reason.
- And if you don't want ever to help this particular person, be clear and concise and leave no openings for further discussion. If he suggests various other ways you could help him, and you just don't want to, tell him, "I'm just too busy (or uncertain of my schedule) to plan ahead right now. I sure hope you can find someone else to help you move out of your mother's house."

It is a skill to be able to turn someone down graciously, and it is a skill worth developing. Just try to remember that anyone who loves you will understand that you can't always do everything for everybody.

I feel like I'm the last on everyone's list of priorities. Is it selfish to want to be first or second, at least occasionally?

Laura, a young mother of three children under the age of seven, put it this way. "I feel so selfish admitting this, but I'm really frustrated: between helping my oldest with homework, getting the middle one to and from preschool and play dates, trying to get the baby on a schedule, keeping up with laundry, and trying to maintain a relationship with my husband, there just doesn't seem to be any time left over for *me*!" If you feel that you are the one who must always keep everyone else in your family functioning, there will naturally be little time or energy left over for taking care of yourself. It's perfectly normal, healthy even, and it's not at all selfish that you want your needs met, too.

We tend to think of mothers as selfless and giving women, people who would rather create a wonderful home and raise high-achieving, considerate, and competent children than pursue their own interests. Truth be told, this cultural ideal creates the conflict. Wanting to be the kind of mother who adores motherhood can make you feel that your first priority should always be someone else. And that can make you feel very selfish if you'd sometimes prefer to read, visit a friend, go to work, or play badminton.

It is not selfish or cause for shame that you would sometimes choose soaking in a fragrant bubble bath to bathing the family dog, or going rock climbing instead of driving your children to their various activities. It is normal and appropriate, at least occasionally, that your own needs should be indulged. You need to be contented as much as any other family member. Taking care of yourself as well as you take care of everyone else shows your children and husband that your needs matter, too. And since your family will not always be as needy of you as they are while your children are little, you also need to maintain your own interests and skills for the future.

I'm sure you've heard the saying that a happy mother means a happy family, and it's true. You must take care of yourself as well as you take care of your family. If you don't, your family will suffer and you will be providing a poor role model for your children. After all, do you really want your husband and children to rely on you so thoroughly that they don't become competent and independent? Do you want to have them think of you as nothing more than a glorified housekeeper? You are not a better wife or mother just because you give all you have to your husband and kids.

The person who takes care of your family should be treated with respect and concern, and this is true even when that person is you. Not only that, but you cannot continue to care adequately for everyone else if you don't also get enough rest and recreation yourself. You will be tired and crabby and that does no one any good. Every member of the family should have responsibilities and also be able to enjoy life, and that includes you. Wanting to be able to take care of your own needs is completely reasonable. That is no cause to feel selfish.

If it's not selfish, then how do I go about meeting my needs as well as the rest of the family's?

Put yourself on your own to-do list. Consider whether or not you are one of those mothers who assume that you must do everything for everyone else. Assess what you truly need to do and what can be delegated to others. Then, when you think about what must get accomplished every day, address your own needs with the same concern and attention that you devote to other demands in your life.

If you believe that to be a good mother you must be responsible for everyone else's happiness, you are in trouble. Mothers are just people. You don't become totally selfless simply because you've given birth, any more than you suddenly become an excellent housekeeper, bookkeeper, chef, baby-sitter, tutor, or ballet dancer. You might be better suited to changing a tire than a baby. Admittedly, mothers often have excellent intuitive powers and are often the best ones in a family to soothe a crabby toddler or to create the perfect grilled cheese sandwich, but other people (most notably fathers, other relatives, and older children) are frequently just as capable of taking care of themselves and each other as is Mom.

Once you've assessed who actually excels at what, start delegating responsibilities accordingly. If your husband is the better cook, let him be the family chef. If you enjoy laundry, then that's your responsibility. As your children mature, give them jobs appropriate to their age and abilities. They will learn important skills, and you future daughters- and sons-in-law will be grateful. When the jobs you don't like or don't do well are passed on to another person, you will have more time and energy to devote to taking care of yourself as well as your family responsibilities, and you will experience the added bonus of less resentment and exhaustion.

No matter what, even if you discover that you are better organized and more skilled at absolutely everything that needs to get done, make sure you give some jobs to others and put yourself and some activities you love on your list of things to do. Even the busiest mothers need time to unwind, time to be pampered and cared for—*especially* the busiest mothers. So include phone calls to your best friends, a walk in the park, time to read, whatever you need to feel whole and at peace with yourself, on your to-do list. Then take the time to do it. The less appealing jobs will get done eventually. Your family will appreciate what you do for them and learn to take care of themselves. And you will feel better.

How can I be the best mom, wife, friend, worker, and daughter without feeling like I have lost myself?

When you are consumed by taking care of everybody else, and by trying so hard to be good at everything, it can be tricky to remember that you are more than simply the roles you fill. If you feel that you are losing yourself in your efforts to be spectacular in each of your various roles, you may be exerting a lot of energy to be something or someone other than what you really are. You need to become clear about what kind of mom, wife, friend, worker, daughter, and really, what kind of person, you are meant to be, and work toward being that person, not toward perfecting your roles.

I would never tell you not to try to lead a productive life, to be less than you are capable of being, but I would tell you to think about what it means to you to be good at everything. Consider how much you personally value and enjoy each segment of your life. If being a highly accomplished, high-energy person comes naturally to you, if doing everything well feels like who you are at your very core, then you will not have *lost* yourself in your attempts to fill all your roles beautifully; you will have found yourself. However, if you experience meeting everyone else's expectations as overwhelming, or if you feel that you will be loved and admired only by being good at all these roles, then you are not being true to yourself, and you will feel lost.

You need to feel that you are a complete person and that you are more than simply what you do, or a composite of roles. You may actually be doing exactly what you want, but are just working too hard to be able to enjoy it. If that's the case, make sure you take breaks and reflect on how you feel. Or you may realize that you are not doing what you want to be doing, that you need more fun or more work or maybe just more sleep in your life to feel complete. Assess what areas give you pleasure and when you feel lost in your roles. Think about times in your life when you've felt truly at peace and what helped you maintain that feeling. Take the time to examine your life and you will be better able to figure out how to find yourself once again.

Consider what is truly important to you. Consider your skills and talents. Have realistic expectations of yourself. Most importantly, put your own needs on your agenda on a daily basis. Maintain friendships that have meaning to you. Spend time each week on things you enjoyed before you had a family.

Think about what you really want and strive for being good enough rather than the best. If you are a good enough mother, your kids will be fine. It you are a good enough friend, or spouse, or daughter, or worker, it will all be fine. If the people you love will love you less because you aren't so perfect, then they really don't love you anyway; they love how you serve their needs. And I'm guessing that you'd much rather them love you for who you are, not for how you care for them. So instead of losing yourself in your efforts to be the best mother or whatever, look toward being good enough and being authentic. The people who *really* love you do so because of who you truly are, not because of some imagined perfection. I think that you can be a better friend, wife, and mother if you *don't* lose yourself.

Put your efforts where you think they need to be. Be a great mom, a great friend, a great daughter, but also be a great you. You will continue to be loved and admired. And you will be able to feel complete.

I am too often impatient or short-tempered. What can I do to increase my patience?

Patience may be a virtue, but many parents find it hard to achieve. High-pitched voices, constant clutter, too many demands on your time, and no time to yourself, which are all common concerns of parents of young children, frazzle the nerves of even the most tolerant among us. However, if you know that you are often unreasonably impatient, you are right to want to try to become less flappable. You probably need to learn to calm yourself down when you feel your patience evaporate so that you can more easily be the parent that you want to be. In addition, if the demands on you are simply beyond your capacity, you may need to change your schedule or get some outside support.

If you feel that your life is manageable but you seem too irritable and impatient, try some well-tested methods to keep calm.

- Whenever you feel impatient, take a deep breath or count to ten (or one hundred) before continuing whatever you were doing. Look at your child (or whoever or whatever it is that is trying your patience so intensely) and think about what you particularly like about him or her. Remember that young children take more time to do many things. Remind yourself that your children are just being children. Sometimes taking the time to reflect on your feelings before acting will allow you to behave more kindly.

- Teach yourself to think before you speak so that you make a conscious choice in how and what you do. When you know you are tired or frustrated or otherwise likely to have less patience, take a moment before opening your mouth. Think about what you want to say before you say anything.

- Leave the room if you find that deep breaths and thinking ahead don't restore your patience or allow you to behave appropriately.

- Whenever you find yourself responding in a less than ideal manner, imagine what your best self would say or do, and then say or do that.

- If trying to be your best self doesn't improve your patience level, pretend that someone you greatly admire is listening to you as you talk to your children, husband, or coworkers. Show this imaginary role model your best efforts at being the calm, well-reasoned, and loving parent or worker you want to be.
- If you feel impatient but manage to behave appropriately, relax and be proud of yourself. You're doing just fine.

When you are stressed by the realities of life, patience may be elusive; patience is often the first thing to go when parents feel overwhelmed and overburdened. If you feel that your needs are rarely met, or simply feel pulled too far in too many directions and that it results in constant impatience and frustration, you may need to simplify your life or find some support.

- If you are juggling too many jobs or roles, you may need to scale back on your responsibilities. Talk with your family and work and determine what you can do to ease your burden. Start delegating tasks that don't absolutely need to be done by you specifically.
- Consider working or volunteering fewer hours or getting more help so that you have more time and don't feel so rushed. Impatience often piggybacks on anxiety about getting everything accomplished; having more time to do what you care about can help ease that sense of time running out on you.
- Simply lowering your standards may help a lot. Become adept at keeping your house a bit less tidy, ordering in meals, or doing laundry less frequently.

- Hire a sitter more often so that you have breaks from routine chores.
- Have family members do more for themselves.
- Learn to say "no" to extra tasks when saying "yes" will overload you.
- Take good care of yourself. Tending to your own needs will allow you to tend to the needs of others with patience and understanding and a clearer head and kinder tongue. Take care of yourself and your patience should return.

You are right to be concerned if you feel impatient much of the time, and it is in your best interests as well as your family's to find a way to take more of your life in stride. You, your work, your mate, and your children all deserve to be treated thoughtfully and well. Take the time to sort everything out if snapping at your loved ones and coworkers has become a bad habit or if it is stress that has caused your patience to fly away. Take time to think before you snap, to get help and support when you need it, and you will handle your life more deftly and pleasantly. You will feel better about yourself, you will be more effective, and those around you will greatly appreciate your even-handed attitude.

How can I learn to tolerate all the noise and demands that seem to accompany my three kids wherever we are?

I think most people leading demanding lives want to get away from the intensity on occasion. Children can provide you with unending love and profound appreciation, but they can also provide you with a whole lot of noise, conflicting needs, dirty dishes, and no privacy. When the volume and chaos rise, it's hard to remember the joy of watching your baby sleeping peacefully, or the warmth of your toddler's hand in yours, and the life of a hermit seems mighty appealing.

When family life has lost all its charms for you, you have two roads toward regaining the desire (or at least willingness) to stay. First, help your children learn to recognize your emotional signals better and know when to calm down, and second, give yourself a break. Here are some tips to help you with each.

First, help your children learn to recognize and respect when you've had enough. If the noise and commotion continue to feel out of control to you, you may not be adequately conveying to your children what is tolerable and what is not. Consider these suggestions:

- When you first feel that you cannot stand the noise much longer, calmly tell your children. *Before* the noise and activity level escalates to terrifying levels, redirect the participants in the bedlam to a quieter activity, another (safe but soundproof) room, or send them outside. Pop in a movie, separate the kids, whatever it takes.

- Recognize that many children need to make noise and get some serious exercise. If you know that you will be at home for an extended period and that your children will need to wriggle and squeal, take them to a park or playground for an hour. Even fast food play spaces, the hallway in a high rise (if the neighbors won't object), or a shopping mall may offer young children enough freedom to get the exercise they need in order to be able to play more quietly once you return home. (Keep in mind that you must be aware of other patrons in public places, so warn your children to run wild and stay within clear geographic limits only in appropriate locations.)

- Learn your children's triggers. If you know what sets them off, what makes them fight, or when they are most likely to get out of control, you can also help them learn to predict when they may need to remove themselves from an activity. When you first hear the beginnings of an argument, for example, interrupt the play with an offer of a snack, read them a story, or put on some dancing music.

- Help your children learn to monitor their own wildness. If you hear things getting out of control, go directly to the kids and point out that they need to calm down. Often kids can't see things spinning out of control as soon as you can; by helping them resolve problems while they are still calm enough to think clearly, you not only get more peace and quiet, you teach them an invaluable skill.

- Plan play dates sensibly. If you know that Elizabeth always gets loud and goofy whenever she plays with Meredith, plan for them to play together only when you know you can take them outdoors or will be in a more tolerant mood.

- Don't agree to an activity if you know it will make you crazy. Personally, I believed that preschool was invented so I didn't have to deal with finger-paints at home. My kids got to finger paint in school, just not at home, and while they may see that as deprivation, I was a much nicer mom as a result. You are allowed to say "no" to things you cannot tolerate.

Second, find ways to take a break. Just as your children deserve to be able to be wild and noisy at times, you deserve to have some peace and quiet.

- Take time to do something you thoroughly enjoy. Instead of doing the grocery shopping on your lunch hour, read a great book or take a nap or a walk.
- Instead of going straight to work (either at home or at your job) after you drop the kids off at school, go for a brisk walk, go to the gym, have a cup of tea, or read a magazine. Give yourself a moment of well-deserved privacy; you'll feel better and be more productive when you return to reality.
- Hire a sitter or swap with a friend. Take your best friends' kids (assuming they are compatible with yours) for a few hours once a week or once a month and have her take yours another day. Plan activities to keep the volume and potential for wildness to a minimum. Your children get play dates, and when your friend has the kids, you get a break.

Living with kids doesn't come easily to everybody; even when you totally adore your children most of the time, the high voices and boisterous behavior can wear on just about anyone. Know yourself and help your children learn to recognize when you've had enough before you get too upset. Help them monitor their own behavior and take breaks when you can. You are not a bad parent for wanting to live a quiet life. You owe it to yourself to help the kids learn to keep their behavior within reasonable limits, and to give yourself mini-vacations, even for only a half hour, so that your love for your children, rather than your frustration with their tumult, is what you and your children experience and remember most.

Am I abnormal that I just didn't find my kids very interesting until they were old enough to smile and respond?

Not too many moms like to admit to finding their infants rather boring, but many parents and grandparents don't find babies all that fascinating. You are certainly not alone in preferring children who interact more. Your job here is twofold: one, don't let your lack of interest lead you to assume that you are a terrible mother, and two, don't let your lack of interest in the early stages of babyhood lead to lack of interest in your kids at all.

Mothers are people, too, although we often have superhuman expectations of ourselves. Being a person means that you have specific tastes and skills, and it would be foolish to think that this wouldn't translate into tastes and skills in mothering. I know several women and men who absolutely adore babies. They will want to hold any baby they encounter, are wonderfully patient and calm with fussy babies, and just thoroughly enjoy that stage. I know just as many parents who, when asked, would admit to preferring their children once they are capable of interaction, who enjoy their children much more once the "dialogue" of smiling at each other and responsive "cooing" begins, or don't really get intrigued by their children until they become more sophisticated toddlers or even school-aged kids.

Ideally, you and your husband and other family members will find different stages of development exciting. If you aren't a baby person, maybe your husband or mother-in-law is. The world is full of lots of different types of people; it's normal to find certain parts of motherhood exciting and others tedious, and it's normal to find it easier to relate to your children at some stages than at others. Be patient, pay attention to your child's changing abilities, and you will find your child more exciting.

Don't worry about not finding your infants too thrilling. As long as you love them and care for them, provide for their needs appropriately and lovingly, it is okay to enjoy some stages more than others. Be open to discovering aspects of every stage that you can enjoy, and accept that you are who you are.

I must include a word of caution, however. Your children need you to be able to be with them, and if you find them not just boring, but somehow unappealing and unacceptable for any noticeable length of time, you need to find out what is causing you to be disinterested in your child. There is a difference between finding some stages, especially the earliest, least interactive weeks of your child's life to be somewhat boring. It is altogether different to be completely indifferent, or to find your child abhorrent. If you find that there is a stage you actually find repugnant, please seek professional help. Both you and your children should be able to delight in each other's company, and if that seems impossible to you, you need to find out why.

Is it awful of me that I was disappointed in the sex of my child?

The truth is that many prospective parents, when totally honest with themselves, long for one sex or the other for a variety of reasons. Some want to have the same sex they are, feeling parent and child will understand each other better or be closer. People who hated their sisters may want boys, or those who felt particularly warmly toward one sibling or another may want a child just like them. Parents who already have children of one sex often wish for the other. They may tell you that they'll be happy as long as the baby is healthy, and they probably will, but that doesn't eliminate the desire for whichever gender they secretly want.

People often find it hard to acknowledge any disappointment in their children; they feel guilty for having wished for a boy and gotten a girl (or the reverse), and worry that their disappointment could make their child feel rejected and unloved. Although many new parents are secretly upset at the sex of their baby, what's important here is that you can get past that disappointment. Face your disappointment and then set about to discover what's wonderful about the child you have.

Whether your child is a boy or a girl, there will be things about him or her that are not what you might have expected. Try to remember that your child is an individual with strengths and weaknesses that are totally his or her own. You will be amazed at some of your child's accomplishments and stymied by others. If you are too invested in your child being a particular way, whether you care too much about attitude, looks, or gender, you will either disappoint yourself further or cause the child to be disappointed in him or herself for not being what you had in mind. Love the true person your child is. You don't want your child to feel that he or she should be something or someone other than that.

Pay attention to the interests, skills, and personality of the child you have. Learn to appreciate what is unique about him. Find enjoyment in the discovery of who he is and wants to become, rather than trying to mold or direct him in the direction of your fantasy child. Once most parents admit to themselves that they'd really wanted the other sex child, they can usually let go of that initial discontent and allow themselves to love the child they have. Then any early disappointment almost automatically turns to delight and you'll all do just fine.

If your disappointment prevents you from enjoying your child, then that can be a problem and you should ask for professional help to understand why you seem unable to bond with your child. You and your child will feel infinitely better when you can wholeheartedly love him or her, regardless of whether he or she was what you expected or wanted. If you can't come to accept and love your child on your own, find a responsible psychotherapist who can help you.

Although in general I think it's good to share lots of your memories with your children about their births, I don't recommend that you tell your daughter that you'd really rather have had a boy, even if you stress to her how much you love her anyway. Many children will then always worry that you are still distressed about their sex. If you were disappointed in the sex of your child but can now fully appreciate what a spectacular and interesting human he or she is, don't worry about having wished for the opposite gender. Just enjoy the child you have and move forward.

One of my kids looks and acts just like my side of the family, while the other looks and acts just like my husband's. I don't love one any more than the other, but am I a bad mom if I just get along more easily with the one that's more like me?

As much as we try to act as if our children are all exactly equal, they are not. Children are just as unique as adults; it's only natural that you have an easier time with one than another. It doesn't mean you should play favorites or that you will love one any more or less than the other. If you are aware of these differences, though, it is also reasonable to worry that your kids might feel the difference in how you relate to each of them, and that this might not be so good.

The reality is that everybody is different, whether they favor your side or your husband's or nobody you've ever known before. There will always be things you adore about each of the people in your life and other traits you could live without. It's okay to recognize that you and your son look alike and have the same sense of humor while your daughter is the spitting image of your husband's Great Aunt Sadie. It's even okay to accept that one child is easier to raise than the other—because that's the truth. The trick is to recognize that what you have or don't have in common is neither more nor less than that. Put no value judgment on these differences and help your children know that easier isn't always better, and that having more in common with one child doesn't lessen the love or enjoyment you have for the other.

To that end, get to know each of them as individuals. Spend time alone with each of your children, preferably doing things of their choosing. Try not to think of either child as a clone of anyone else; acknowledge that each child shares some the parents' physical, personality, and mental traits, but each also has other aspects that are uniquely his or hers. Your children are not just replications of you or your husband; they are distinctive and one of a kind. Getting to know and love each of your kids and appreciating them for their many qualities, both similar to and opposite to yours, will alleviate any guilt you may have about finding one easier, and will eliminate any anxiety, yours or your children's, that you may love one more.

I hate to admit this, but I have a favorite child. What should I do?

As much as we try to love every child equally, parents don't always succeed. After all, your children are all different. Sometimes one parent simply seems to get along exceedingly well with one of the children, or finds one of the kids to be more appealing than the others. What's important is that they all feel well loved, and that you treat the children as if you clearly love them all enormously.

A friend asked Diana, a wise mother of three kids, if she had a favorite. Diana knew each of her children very well and enjoyed the differences among them. While one might be more challenging than the others, Diana found meeting those challenges to be very exciting. She felt that she learned something and enjoyed something different with each of her kids, and that she could honestly say that she loved her children very, very much, and very differently.

I think this is an excellent strategy for child rearing and for dealing with those feelings that you might favor one child over another. You are bound to find certain traits more appealing than others, and to think that the easy child, the neediest child, or the more conventionally talented child might be favored. But loving a child involves many aspects of your personality as well as your children's. You may favor certain aspects of each child at different times in your lives.

I know a family of six children in which each child believed that he or she was the favorite for a time and their mother admitted that this was true. That served to make some of the children feel more secure, knowing that they would be the favorite at some point, and if they weren't favored for a time, they knew their turn would come. Unfortunately, others found it distressing. The rotating favoritism made the less confident kids uncomfortable knowing that they could lose that favored spot at any time or unseat the current champ. It also seemed to add to the competitiveness among the kids. The more sensitive kids in this family would much rather have felt loved unconditionally and not have anyone be favored.

Showing favoritism is far worse than if a parent feels a different kind of love for each child. No matter what, please treat each child fairly and with love, regardless of whether or not you have a favorite. You may certainly feel differently about each child, and you can even treat them differently as long as each gets what he or she needs and feels that you are fair and loving to them all.

What's important is to love each child for who he or she truly is, not for making you proud, making your life easier, or for following in your footsteps. I believe that if you seek to understand who your child is and who he wants to become, you will love what is essential about him and he will thrive. You will also be able to have all of your children be loved enough not to worry about playing favorites. When you seek to know your children, to honor what is real about them, even if they oppose your views, have different interests or skills, or are a bit of a handful, they will feel adequately loved and you will come to love them in plentiful and similar amounts. Realistically, love is not something that should or can be quantified. Love each child, be fair, and it will be okay.

I devoted everything I had emotionally to my firstborn. What can I do to stop feeling so bad that my second and third aren't getting as much?

It's hard to give as much individual attention to second or other subsequent children, but that doesn't translate into those children getting less. There are advantages and disadvantages to each birth order position. While firstborns may be the center of their parents' universe, seconds and thirds grow up learning to share, to be patient, and they always have a peer group. You gave your firstborn what you were able to give, and he undoubtedly benefited from your undivided attention and nurturing. But subsequent children also profit from your calmer, more experienced approach.

What you gave to your first was different, certainly, but it wasn't necessarily better. Try to come to terms with the concept that different doesn't suggest either better or worse. It's natural that the first child has the most detailed and organized photo album, was taken on more field trips, or had more brand new toys, because, with no other children, your focus is directed only on him. With the other children, you must spread your attention and resources across them all. But again, that isn't bad; it's just different.

If you still believe that you have shortchanged the younger children, you can make some efforts at reparation. Spend time, one on one, with each child, preferably on a regular basis. Take the middle child out to lunch once a week, go to the movies with the youngest, or institute a regular activity—a board game, bedtime reading, cooking dinner together—whatever appeals to each of you that you can do together, just the two of you. Your first child may have had you all to himself when he was a baby, but you can still have high quality and individual time with younger children. You have a lifetime to be a great parent; to spend time with your children. Enjoy your children, spend time with them, but don't count or compare the hours you spend with each.

When you are feeling particularly bad about your younger children, try thinking about what they have gained by being born later in your parenting life. Younger children learn to be more adaptable, they are exposed to a variety of activities, often at a younger age than the first, because they tag along, they generally have parents who are calmer and more confident (and occasionally more financially stable), and their older siblings often are expected to be more responsible and higher achieving than they are.

Every position in a family has its good and not-so-good points. As long as you give each child what he or she needs, you can be proud of your parenting. Your younger children won't suffer because they didn't have you all to themselves.

Is it terrible that now that there's another child in the family, I vacillate between feeling guilty that I can no longer be so totally focused on my first child and feeling annoyed with her for wanting more of me than I have left over to give?

No, it's *reasonable* to miss being able to devote yourself completely to your firstborn while at the same time feeling resentful about the difficult demands she makes on you. Ambivalence is normal; it may not be pleasant, but it is normal.

Your life is different with two small children than with just one. With only one child, you had only her to consider, and all your child-rearing attention logically went to her. You both became accustomed to her being the center of your universe, and now that has to change. With that change comes some regret about no longer being able to be so completely devoted to her, as well as some resentment that she's not somehow suddenly totally independent and gracious about giving up your previously totally undiluted commitment to her.

With two or more children of different ages, it's often hard to take care of everybody's needs as thoroughly and efficiently as when there was just one child. It seems to me that the hardest part about becoming a mother the first time has to do with your changing identity and priorities. What's challenging about becoming a mother the second time is you have to learn to juggle the emotional and practical needs of each child as well as your own.

Accept that you just can't give your undivided attention to everyone in the family at the same time. Part of growing up, for both you and your children, is realizing your own personal limitations and being realistic about what you can and can't do. If you used to spend long hours with your firstborn, understand that losing that time alone together is tough on both of you.

- Show your firstborn that you love her just as much as ever by spending time together when the other child is napping.
- Show her how taking care of a younger child is different than taking care of her. Point out that you take her to her school or help her with homework while you diaper her sister.
- Show her photos of herself at her sister's age, getting the same kind of loving attention her sister gets now.
- If she seems interested, engage her help in caring for the younger child. Even a two-year-old can go get a blanket for the baby, and older children often feel very good about being able to read to younger children or the like. *Do not make her into a second mother* or expect her to be a baby-sitter while the kids are still young. You want her to help out because it will make her feel special, more capable, and competent; her helping is not intended to ease your load but to support her, so if it doesn't appeal to her, don't push her.

- Make sure that you have some one-on-one time with each child.
- Talk about what you like about having more than one child and how it is fun to have a sibling—or how much fun it will be when the baby is old enough to play with her.

Accept that there will be times when you desperately miss being able to care for just one child and times when you love taking care of more. Help your child understand that each child has something unique to add to the family, and that loving or focusing a lot of time on one doesn't diminish the love you have for the other. And remember that actions speak much louder than words, especially the younger the child. Show her you still adore her by taking time alone with her, by giving her special privileges (reserved for her more "mature" abilities), and by telling her how glad you are that she exists.

Should I feel guilty that I just don't especially like my six-year-old?

When Tina's child was seven, she said, "If I were to walk into a room filled with people, my son would be the last one I'd choose to be with." Now that her son is in college, they are very close. Tina worked hard to get to know her son, to understand what made him so challenging to raise, and in the process, Tina began to appreciate him for all of his wonderful qualities and was able to focus less on what she found to be somewhat irritating ones. It's sad, of course, when a mother feels so distant and unconnected to her own child, but this happens more than you might imagine.

Some kids just don't suit their moms or dads. Mothers who want frilly, feminine, and docile daughters may recoil if their real daughters are aggressive tomboys. Families that value intellectual pursuits above all else may be bewildered and uncomfortable with a child whose greatest talents and passions are athletic. A child who seems "easy" to me may be terrifying to you, or the reverse. But you get the children you get. Ideally, you will love them, and learn to like them, too.

In addition, some parents just do much better when their children are certain ages. Everybody's heard of the "terrible twos," and many parents dread having their children become temporary miniature dictators. Personally, I loved when my kids were that age; I found their certainty and drive toward independence fascinating rather than frustrating. Similarly, lots of parents consider getting their own apartments when their previously charming school-aged children become teenagers, yet some parents find this to be their favorite age. Your discomfort with your son or daughter now may be temporary.

What's most important is to maintain a loving relationship with your kids, regardless of how difficult or surprising they become. Often, the times when our children's personalities are the least appealing are when they need our unconditional love and support the most. It's okay not to like everything about your child, and it's even okay to find your kid somewhat unappealing. Just be sure to be constantly aware of your behavior, show the child as much patience and understanding as you can muster, and treat her well. Even if you have nothing beyond blood and a shared home in common, learn who he or she is and what he or she's all about. Treat him or her with respect and love, and the rest should fall into place. Before you know it, you may find that you really like each other after all.

If no matter how hard you try to like your child you still find her unbearable, or if you are unable to behave lovingly toward her, please consider getting professional help. While having bad feelings about someone you love happens to everyone occasionally, you and your child deserve to have a closer, less antagonistic relationship. If your child's behavior is actively off-putting, your job is to help him or her become more socially graceful and appealing. If there is just a personality clash that never lets up, you need to find a way to bridge that abyss between you. If there is something about you or your own childhood that prevents you from feeling good about your son or daughter, you need to work that through so that your child isn't hurt by your issues from the past. Get counseling, either alone or with your child, and work through whatever concerns are preventing you from enjoying each other.

If you treat your child lovingly and try to get to know her more personally, chances are good that she'll either outgrow whatever behaviors you find so unattractive or you will grow to like her as well as you love her. If you can't provide her an appropriately loving and accepting home, get some help. Your son or daughter deserves to be brought up in an atmosphere that's tolerant and loving, and you deserve to feel comfortable about your relationship. You both should be able to feel at ease and accepting of yourselves and each other, and if you can't do that on your own, therapy or counseling can help.

Should I feel guilty that I really don't like my child's friends?

There are three likely reasons for your discomfort with your child's friendships. Most of the time, when a parent doesn't like a child's friends, the problem is that the parent feels that the friends are a "bad influence" on their child; you know, those kids who are always getting into trouble. In some situations, on closer examination, the unlikable friend appears to be a perfectly acceptable child, just more advanced socially with more independence than you as the parent are ready to afford your own child. In other families, the parents don't like one or another of their child's friends because of a personality clash.

Figure out what the real issue is here. Ask yourself the following questions:

- Is your child's friend a conscientious student, one who doesn't get into trouble?
- Is your child's friend honest and trustworthy?
- Is your child's friend socially more advanced?
- Does your child's behavior change when he or she is with this friend?
- Have your child's grades dropped since the friendship began?
- Has your child's behavior become problematic since this friendship?
- Does your child seem secretive about this friendship?
- Does the other child have more freedom, fewer rules than you allow your child?
- Do you have a relationship with the other child's parents?
- Are the kids supervised at the other child's home?
- Are you worried that this child will push your child to do things he or she (or you) isn't ready for?
- Do you feel that the other child is somehow exploiting, bullying, or hurting your child?
- Do you like this child's personality?

When you consider the above questions, it should become clearer to you whether your concerns are that the friendship isn't healthy for your child, you are uncomfortable with your own child's increasing need for independence, or you just don't really like this particular kid. Try to be completely honest with yourself. It would be very easy not to be ready for how mature and independent your child is becoming, but to interpret your discomfort as justifiable concern that this other child is bad for your kid. Once you determine what the real problem is, you can start to fix it.

- If this friend is truly a bad influence, you have every right to limit the friendship.
- Make sure that the kids hang out at your house when they get together, and make sure you are always home.
- Offer to drive the kids and oversee the activity when they need to go anywhere.
- Help your child maintain friendships with other kids.
- Don't give permission for your child to do anything that you are convinced may lead to trouble.

One clever mother who thought her children were getting into a rough crowd took a creative approach to the dilemma. She kept her children very busy. She made lots of family plans, such as going to museums and the theater or visiting relatives to limit the time her kids had available to spend with the "bad influences." The kids saw far less of the unsavory potential troublemakers, and as a bonus had a number of culturally enriching experiences.

If your child is ready for more freedom though, and the friend is simply a bit farther along the road to independence, then it may be time for you to start to ease up. Talk to more seasoned parents. Find out what behaviors are the norms for kids your child's age in your neighborhood. If truly everyone goes to afternoon movies without an adult chaperone, it may be time to let your child go, too—despite your uneasiness. Holding your child back can make him feel that you don't trust him, lead to rebellion, or social isolation. If he's ready to be more grown up, then you may need to get yourself ready, too. Your job as a parent is to support and nurture your child's growth and maturation, to help them develop good judgment and lead productive lives. It is not to shelter them unnecessarily.

If you just don't like this kid but both children are doing well in school, are pleasant and polite most of the time, and stay out of trouble, then just try to keep your feelings to yourself. Children do have distinct personalities from a very early age and you are not going to like everybody that your child likes. Your child probably doesn't like all of your friends, either. As long as you are pleasant and polite to your child's friend and can manage to keep your more negative feelings about her to yourself, you can relax.

Having your children grow up and develop friendships of their own is wonderful, but it can also be very nerve-racking. You want your children to choose friends of whom you approve, to have interests in which you can share, and to stay close to you always. Yet you also want them to grow up and be able to live on their own successfully. Making friends is part of growing up; not all children develop friendships with people their parents like.

You may believe that you want your child to become independent, but your child's independence is often more attractive in theory than in practice. Many parents resist the child's autonomy when those autonomous choices, in the form of unappealing friends, come over to visit. Try to keep in mind that in a perfect world, what you're looking for is what's best for your child, including friends with whom he can develop and grow safely and positively. If you use good judgment about your children's choices, intervening only when necessary, recognizing your own resistance to your child's pushing for independence, and keeping your own personality issues in check, then you have nothing to feel guilty about.

I can't even say this out loud, but is something wrong with me that I don't think my own kids are attractive?

Some parents may just be more objective than others. While most parents think that their own offspring are unequalled in looks, intelligence, athleticism, and charm, others are capable of more objectivity. Being able to see your children through unprejudiced eyes is difficult for many, but it is not impossible, nor is it necessarily bad to be somewhat clear-eyed about your own kids.

What's interesting to me is how some parents can be totally objective about some of their children's traits and completely starry-eyed or hypercritical about others. And it seems that the aspects of their children's personality or appearance that are either delightful or worrisome usually say more about the parent than about the children. What's important here isn't so much whether or not you find your children attractive, but more about how your opinion effects your behavior toward them.

As long as your perception of their looks has few practical implications, your kids will be fine. However, if you care deeply about appearances, if you find your own children so unappealing that it hurts you to look at them, or if your impression of their lack of beauty leads you to constantly trying to "help" them to look better, then you need to do some soul searching and probably seek professional help in order to avoid crushing your child's self-esteem or passing along your personal issues. While it's okay to find your children less than gorgeous, it is *not* okay to make them uncomfortable about certain body parts, facial characteristics—or really anything about themselves.

If you focus too much on any one aspect of your children to the exclusion of all others, your children will think that trait is what is most important in life. Rather than worry that you don't find your children too attractive, think about what you *do* like about your kids. Take time to listen to them; ask them about their interests. Focus on their strengths and keep in mind that your children's definition of their own strengths is every bit as important as yours.

If you support them in their interests and abilities, your children will thrive. If you dwell on their less appealing characteristics, they will worry that they aren't somehow good enough for you. If, after thinking about it, you can't get past tormenting yourself about how unattractive you find your own kids, get counseling support. You may have unresolved issues about your own appearance or your husband's, or about some other part of your life that won't allow you to be the kind of loving and accepting parent you want to be.

In my work, I am fortunate to get to know people of every age and background, of a variety of interests and abilities. What has become very clear to me is that there are many definitions of beauty, many types of intelligence, and countless ways to be a valuable, interesting, smart, appealing, and lovable person. Everyone is good enough at something; everyone has wonderful qualities. It is up to you as a parent to find the lovable aspects of your children, to accept, but not focus on, the less attractive parts, whatever they are, and if you are too stuck on the so-called negative parts of your kids, to get help for yourself so that you can be the loving parent your kids deserve.

I hate going to my kids' recitals and games. What's wrong with me?

Not all parents love attending their children's recitals, games, or school events. But if you love your children, you go with a smile on your face and the resolve to pay attention and shower your child with superlatives. If you don't know how to go to one of these activities without betraying your true feelings about them, follow these basic rules for parental attendance at important children's events:

- Don't gripe about going, not before, during, or after.
- Don't make fun of or criticize the program or any of the kids in the show or on the team.
- Don't criticize the coach or teacher.
- Try to look as if you want to be there. Have fun.
- Do not embarrass your child, either by clapping, cheering, booing too loudly, or showing poor sportsmanship.
- Don't take photos during the performance or game unless it is specifically allowed and will not distract the kids.
- Rather than give your assessment of how things went, ask your child what he thought about it.
- If your child makes errors or performs poorly, be prepared to listen and help your child deal with his feelings about what happened. Sometimes what parents see as a poor performance the child sees as completely acceptable.
- Never criticize or belittle your child for his lack of perfection. Help the child learn from the experience; don't equate the child with the event.
- Always be respectful of your child's interest, despite the fact that you don't share it.

Even if your child messes up, or if the show is objectively pretty pathetic, your job as parent is to be your child's support, and support doesn't necessarily mean you have to enjoy the specifics of the display or offer praise for a job well done. What your child needs from you is the assurance that you care about him and that you value his efforts and enthusiasm. Whether your child strikes out in the last inning or plays the Tchaikovsky *Violin Concerto* perfectly at age six, he needs to know that you love *him*, not his accomplishments. You want him to feel good about himself, know that you think he's just swell no matter what, and that you are proud that he is an involved participant.

What that all boils down to is this: you must appreciate your child for the wonderful and interesting person he is, and if he is involved in activities that require an audience, you need to be there. You don't have to love every minute, but you need to show pride in your child's efforts, whatever their outcome. So while it is okay to find these events somewhat tedious, you must also learn to appreciate your child's involvement in them, and be there, lovingly, to cheer him on.

My child has a lot of problems, which has caused me great disappointment and cost us lots of money. What can I do so that I don't feel so resentful that he isn't more "normal?"

When your kids are troubled, you are troubled. It is a rare parent who *never* faces difficult or stressful times with her kids, but it is also true that some children have more than their share of problems. When your child struggles constantly, whether with physical, intellectual, or psychological issues, it is a drain on you emotionally and financially, and it would be unusual if you didn't occasionally feel a bit resentful, disappointed, or exhausted. Although your resentment might be understandable, your child needs you to get past it.

When you decided to become a mother, you had certain expectations about what your kids would be like. Maybe you imagined that they would be funny, clever, tall, or red-headed. Maybe you conjured up images of singing duets with them or having them follow your career path. All parents must face that the children they bring into the world may or may not resemble their fantasy children, and they must learn to love and appreciate how their children are different from and similar to those fantasies.

Despite objectively understanding that no one is perfect, parents often expect their own children to be just that. When facing a child with chronic problems, coming to terms with that reality can be that much more challenging. Not only do you need to become comfortable and accepting of your child's unexpected limitations, you must also give up the notion of the life you'd anticipated with your child.

Elizabeth's daughter was quite ill when she was very young, causing Elizabeth to quit her job in order to care for her. Although grateful that she was available for her child and thrilled that her little girl ultimately recovered and is now quite robust, she lost several years of career opportunities and income. Taking so much time off work was just not what she had envisioned for herself, and she had never imagined the stress of caring for a sick child. Elizabeth resented the time and effort spent, and that resentment colored her relationship with her daughter for a long time.

If your resentment seems omnipresent, if you feel you can't get away from it or that it negatively impacts your relationship with your child, please seek professional help. Your child cannot help being who he is. No child wants to have problems. In addition to obtaining help for yourself, get help for your child. While it is completely understandable that your child's problems are wearing you down, there is help out there to get you both through it. Make sure for your sake as well as your child's that you get the support you each need so that you and your whole family can lead a contented life.

We are so much more relaxed and lenient with our second child. Is it totally unfair to our first?

Your first child got lots of individual attention that your second child didn't, and the second gets more relaxed parents. Everyone gets something special, something beneficial. You were doing the best you possibly could do for your first, and now that you have some experience, you are doing the best you can do for the second, which may include being more relaxed. This is what happens in many, many families. The trick is to let yourself off the hook for being human.

Lots of parents enter parenthood worried that they will make some terrible mistake that will ruin their perfect child's life. They focus on every minor detail of the first child's poop when he's a baby, verbal skills as a toddler, and his academic, athletic, or social accomplishments as he continues to grow. Once the second child arrives, the parents' attention is divided, milestones seem less monumental, and the parents begin to relax, more confident that they and their offspring will likely all do okay.

But the first child is, and always will be, the first. Every new stage he or she goes through is new to the parents as well. This uncharted territory takes a different kind of vigilance and creates a particular parental kind of anxiety. I'm not saying that this is good, mind you; just that it is understandable and common. So much so that a dear friend of mine has said on more than one occasion that the first child is "the screw-up kid," not because the kids makes mistakes, but because the firstborn is the one we, the parents, make all (well, many) of our mistakes on.

So feeling guilty that you are a more relaxed, lenient parent to your second child than you were to your first is hardly unusual. However, guilt about that is rarely useful, so if you feel really bad, instead of stewing in your guilty juices, apologize to your firstborn and, if there is still time (and I believe there always is) change your ways. When you start to rein in the first, remind yourself that she has excellent judgment and good friends, and let her go. If you are actually too lenient with the second, tighten things up a bit.

It's okay to handle your children differently if their behavior or circumstances warrant it, but you will do your best parenting when you suit the limits to the child and the situation, not so much to your personal mental state. This means that if you believe you have been too anxious or strict in the past, you loosen up, but only if loosening up seems to meet your child's needs. Don't eliminate a curfew for your twelve-year-old simply because you never let your fourteen-year-old out of the house. Limits still have value; they just need to be tailored to the needs of the situation and people involved.

Good parents continue to assess their parenting skills and styles as long as they are parents. Analyze what each child needs, and to the best of your ability, provide it. You can't go back and change the past, but you can use your experience and perspective to be a better parent—to both children—in the future. If you do, you have nothing to feel bad about because you will be the best parent you can be. You can't really do more than that, can you?

Chapter Three

Motherhood and Marriage

Before Nicole and Tyler had children, their lives were pretty straightforward. They had only themselves and each other to consider. Household tasks, such as who did the laundry, cleaned the bathroom, did the banking, or made the meals, were divided up and shared, and there was usually plenty of time left over to relax and enjoy each other's company. On weekends, they could stay up together all night to watch the sun rise the next morning, and they had loads of time to talk about their hopes and dreams. They could be romantic, sexy, and spontaneous; some weeknights they would get dressed up and go out; weekends they could stay home naked in bed all day if they wanted. They could choose whether to go out to dinner with friends, take in a movie, go to clubs, or spend lots of time alone, and still have time and energy left over to focus on each other.

Once children entered their family, though, all that changed. The chores around the house increased exponentially. Nicole started doing laundry several times a week, the mess and clutter never disappeared, and they each had less vigor to deal with it all. They discovered that when they stay up all night now, it's usually because one of the kids is sick or fussy, and they can't sleep in together the next morning because the kids demand their constant attention. If they want to see a movie or visit with friends, they must arrange for a baby-sitter. Nicole sadly admits that she doesn't feel very sexy anymore; they rarely seem to get dressed up, and there isn't enough time in the day to take a break for herself, let alone to pay attention to Tyler. Life with children changed their marriage dramatically.

Many marriages experience tremendous stress and change when children are born, but this is not to say that there aren't many benefits to having children. Lots of women are totally charmed when they witness the nurturing sides of their husbands; it's very endearing when your partner cuddles your crying baby for hours while you get to catch up on your sleep. Creating children together, providing them with a home and loving parents, and watching them grow and mature brings many couples closer. No one else on earth cares about your kids as much as you and your kids' dad, and that total commitment and concern about your kids forges a strong bond.

But there is no doubt that maintaining your marriage as a marriage, not just as copartners, is a challenge. Seeing yourselves as loving and romantic and being able to nurture each other while you also nurture your children takes effort. And while even the most devoted couple sometimes has difficulty putting forth that effort, it is necessary—and absolutely worth it.

Child rearing is very consuming; it takes up much of your married life while the kids are growing up. But if you think about it, the ultimate goal in raising kids is for them to become independent and capable adults, which means that they will eventually leave home, and you and your mate will be alone together once again. Most couples, if they even bother to consider the seemingly distant time in their future when their last kid moves out, hope and expect that they will still have something in common, things to talk about other than their kids, and will actually continue to want to be together. But if you don't nurture your marriage while you are raising your kids, you may not have much of a marriage left when you find yourselves alone together again.

Being alert and aware of your own and each other's attitudes and needs is difficult to manage when you are focused on the children, but it is critical to the future of your marriage. Many couples, particularly those who had strong relationships before they had children, take each other for granted once they have kids. They think that because their marriage has a solid foundation they don't need to attend to it so closely. But you can think of your marriage as you think of your home. Just because it has a solid foundation doesn't mean it doesn't require routine maintenance. Occasionally, structural damage becomes evident and major renovation is required. With a marriage, as with a house, it's better to solve problems while they are small. Otherwise, they can become so costly or overwhelming that the best solution is just to get out.

Lots of couples are so dedicated to taking care of their children, home, and jobs that they don't take care of themselves or each other. It seems to me that the best way to ensure that your marriage stays a marriage, not just a partnership in parenthood, is to work on it *now*. Working on your relationship regularly can lead you to have a more satisfying marriage not only now, while you are bringing up your children, but in the future as well.

Did you know that, typically, couples with young children kiss their children more often than they kiss each other? While the kids are young, moms and dads give and receive more physical affection from their kids than from each other; they allow their roles as romantic partners to take a backseat to their roles as parents. What does that do to a marriage? Is it good for either the kids or the marriage?

Often, putting your parenting first seems logical—noble, even. After all, you are adults; you are capable of delaying gratification of your needs in order to nurture your children. If it leads to ignoring your marriage, though, putting the kids first all the time actually puts the them in an inappropriate and uncomfortable position. Kids want their parents to love each other. They want to be important to their parents, but they don't want to be the only reason their parents stay together; that puts a terrible burden on them. Kids who feel that their parents have nothing in common beyond the kids often worry about their parents' marriage. They may feel "too important" to their parents. They may worry about how their parents will react to anything they do or make choices in their own lives based more on their perceptions of their parents' needs or wishes than on their own talents or interests. When a family is too child-centric, the kids may not learn how a loving and nurturing family balances and meets the needs of both parents and children.

When parents focus exclusively on the kids, they also often lose their ability to focus on each other, and that distance between them makes it harder for them to share their personal issues, solve problems as a couple, or work things out when their attitudes or priorities are at odds with one another. They forget how to work together, they don't develop a unified approach to parenting, and they don't have each other's support while dealing with either the complications or the joys of life. Couples must learn to remain close while they are parenting so that their closeness will continue long past the days when those sweet, adorable, and demanding youngsters need their constant attention.

This chapter focuses on how having children impacts your relationship. Couples who become parents together are faced with many challenges: how to coordinate and unify their attitudes about child rearing, how to spend their limited leisure time, how to divide up household chores, who should make the money, and who gets to decide how to spend it. They need to figure out how to have fun together as a couple and as a family, how to be supportive of one another, and how to nurture each other and themselves while raising great kids.

All too often, parents allow their parenting roles to become overwhelming. They become so consumed with the practicalities of raising a family that they don't take the time to nurture their marriage. They take each other for granted, they forget to be polite and loving toward the person they've chosen to spend their whole lives with, and then they feel guilty about it.

This chapter should help parents remember to take care of themselves and their relationships. It looks at the problems couples face when children enter their relationships, whether the couple is married or cohabitating, heterosexual or gay. For the sake of convenience, the couple is generally referred to as husband and wife, but often the issues are the same regardless of their marital or sexual status.

In this chapter you will find ideas to help you maintain the closeness in your relationship, reassurance that many of the tensions between you are common, and suggestions as to getting outside help when you need it—whether that means a housekeeper or a marriage counselor. This chapter also examines the many stresses, emotions, and behaviors that couples experience when they have children and helps you maintain or fine-tune your marriage so that you and your mate will still want to be together when the children leave home.

My husband and I are both so busy just with getting through each day; I feel guilty that we seem to have no energy left for each other. How can we make our marriage a priority again?

Just as you need to spend time with your children, you need to focus on your marriage. When marriage is put on the backburner for too long, it either burns up or evaporates, leaving you with little in common beyond your children and memories of when you cared for and made time for each other.

You can make your marriage a priority again by making it clear to each other that this is your mutual goal. Take care of yourself so that you have more energy, and devote actual time and thought to your marriage. Remember, all relationships need nourishment. Find ways to improve your energy level and available time:

- Reassess your priorities. What do you consider the most important things you do each day? What can you do less frequently or thoroughly? If you don't exhaust yourself attending to unimportant (or at least relatively less important) jobs, and if you set clear priorities, manage the essentials, and relax your standards about the rest, you'll have more time and enthusiasm to devote to your spouse.
- If you still don't have the stamina to keep up with all your various roles and responsibilities, even after you've eliminated the unnecessary, find some support. Hire a housekeeper if at all possible, or enlist a friend to help; swap baby-sitting for cooking or cleaning for each other. Delegate tasks to coworkers or your kids whenever appropriate. You don't have to do everything yourself; ask for assistance if you need it!

❧ Pay attention to your physical well-being. Eat healthfully and get enough sleep and exercise. A well-timed, nutritious snack or catnap can give you the extra energy you need to finish a project or stay up a bit later; exercise, even if it entails taking a five-minute walk or using the stairs instead of the elevator at work, helps decrease depression and increase energy.

Devote some conscious effort toward strengthening your marriage:

❧ Take time to be together. Do things as a couple. Take a walk together or chat on the phone or online daily, if that will allow more privacy. Schedule time for the two of you, especially if your habit has been to take care of everyone else first, and do not give that time to anyone else. If someone asks you to go out on your only night alone, tell him or her that you have plans, because you do.

❧ Listen to each other without interruptions from anyone or anything, including the children, pets, or telephone calls. Show interest and be sincere.

❧ Show your appreciation of how hard each of you works. Say "please" and "thank you" whenever appropriate.

❧ Make time for physical as well as emotional intimacy. Send your kids on a sleepover at a friend's house or to Grandma's for the weekend.

❧ Be honest and clear about your interests and goals—for your children, for yourself, and for your marriage—and share these with your partner, even when they are different than they used to be or if you fear that your mate won't agree with you. Knowing what's truly important to each of you allows you to achieve your goals and brings you closer together.

- ☞ If you and your mate make an important decision that you later regret, make changes. You can change your mind about many things, including where you work or where you live or how you spend your time. Make sure that what you do individually, as a couple, and as a family accurately reflects your values and allows you to enjoy your lives together.

- ☞ If it seems that you and your mate do not share some essential goals and values, work toward finding agreeable compromises. Talk about your differences, listening respectfully to each other. Keep an open mind.

- ☞ Be kind to each other. Hug each other; kiss your mate hello, good-bye, good morning, and good night. Hold hands again. Offer back rubs.

You make your marriage a priority by safeguarding time together, being honest with each other about what you are thinking, and by being kind, loving, and respectful. Don't let your confidence in your relationship make you believe that continued effort isn't necessary. Take care of your partner and make sure he takes care of you.

Sometimes when I feel frustrated or angry with the kids or work, I find myself starting an argument with my husband. Why do I do that when I know whatever upset me isn't his fault?

It sounds like it's hard for you to allow yourself to express anger, even when it's appropriate, toward your children. Unfortunately, not expressing your anger doesn't make it disappear, so you unintentionally create a situation allowing you to "justifiably" dump it on your husband. You may feel good that you don't explode at your children, but you feel bad that your husband inappropriately catches the brunt of your fury.

Misdirecting your most negative emotions toward your partner may protect your children from witnessing you losing your temper, but it doesn't teach them that anger is a normal and acceptable response to many situations, nor does it help them understand that you can love someone very much and still get angry with them. So unless you're at risk for raging at them uncontrollably, holding those unpleasant emotions back isn't doing them any real favors. In families as in life, people do things that annoy others or hurt their feelings, often inadvertently. Expressing anger appropriately when your children have broken rules or behaved carelessly or inconsiderately teaches them that their behavior has consequences, and that loving people also feel anger. Showing your annoyance and then resolving or recovering from those bad feelings helps children learn to manage their own feelings successfully.

In addition, you create unnecessary tensions and discomfort in your marriage if you manufacture conflict and argue because you are really misdirecting your anger toward your husband. Just because he loves you doesn't mean he'll put up with you treating him badly forever. Feeling loved and emotionally safe makes family life enjoyable; if your spouse is constantly starting arguments or being picky or overly critical for no apparent reason (or because he or she is actually upset with the kids or his or her boss), eventually, the unpleasant behaviors may erase all memories of the loving relationship you once shared.

It's important to show anger and irritation when those emotions make sense and to direct those emotions to the person or persons who caused them. By sharing negative feelings constructively, your children learn to treat others well and to handle their own emotions positively. When you respond appropriately to those unpleasant feelings, you get over them much faster, allow opportunities for resolving conflict, and do not shift your anger toward an innocent person. You feel better faster, your kids learn to manage their emotions, and your husband no longer has to receive your misguided fury. That works out well for everybody.

If knowing all this, you still can't figure out how to show your children that you are upset in a safe, comfortable way, then your issues with anger may run too deep. Please seek professional support. Although many women have trouble handling anger in general and anger toward loved ones in particular, you will feel better if you are able to manage your anger successfully. Your kids and husband will benefit, too. When you are comfortable that you can safely and constructively express the whole spectrum of emotions, from joy to rage, you can all live your lives without fear that your emotions will get the best of you.

Now that we have children, my husband and I no longer divide up all the housekeeping, child care, and financial responsibilities equally. What can I do about feeling guilty for not contributing as much income, and resentful that he's not doing as much around the house?

Many marriages that start out to be quite egalitarian change dramatically once children enter the picture. Household tasks multiply, who works how many hours outside the home sometimes changes, and income often diminishes. Regardless of whether the mother continues her paid employment, even in the twenty-first century, she typically becomes responsible for the bulk of the housework and child care. For many women who prided themselves on their feminist relationships before parenthood, this turn of events hurts.

Who does the laundry or takes out the garbage takes on political significance in many families. Even when their husbands are working many hours outside the home while they provide the child care, moms who find themselves always the one to call the baby-sitter, change diapers, and do the grocery shopping, laundry, and cooking can become uncomfortable. They fear that they have given up their freedom or equality, or maybe that they are letting other women down by assuming such gender stereotypical roles. They also worry that if they are the ones doing all the house and child-oriented work, they will lose power in the marriage and provide a poor role model for their children.

When it gets right down to it, I don't think that it is all that important who does what around the house. I know of couples that have elaborate systems to make sure that each family member does his or her equal and non-gender-related share of household and child-care tasks, and others who divide roles along very traditional lines. Happiness is not guaranteed in either situation. What matters most is that you and your husband do the things that need to be done, and that you both feel that your time is well spent and appreciated.

If equality matters to you, if you feel less respected and have less self-respect when you alone do what has commonly been considered "women's work," then divide the jobs in your household differently. Audrey and Alfredo, working parents of four-year-old twins, use a job chart. They list all the things that need to be taken care of on a daily and weekly basis and divide the jobs up, taking turns with which one does which half of the list. One month Audrey does all kitchen and laundry jobs while

Alfredo tackles the yard and bill paying, and the next month they switch. Other couples simply divide the jobs according to each other's interests, skills, and time available—one always washing dishes, managing homework, and supervising baths, the other always doing the heavy cleaning, car maintenance, and laundry. You and your husband must find ways to take care of your family that work for you and that you feel reflect what you value.

I am home with the kids far more than my husband is, but he wants to be as involved in parenting as possible. He's trying to be a good dad, and I feel a little guilty admitting it, but I kind of like it when I'm fully in charge. How can we share parenting decisions without my feeling resentful that he's not more available, or undermined when he is more actively involved?

When a husband works particularly long hours or often has overnight business trips, a wife may understandably feel that she is the primary parent, the one who makes all the family decisions while Dad is unavailable, and she may grow to like it. When the father reenters the family, it can feel somewhat intrusive. Ellen described feeling as if her husband was butting in when he expressed his opinions about the kids. While he was away, she made all the decisions about everything, and she enjoyed it; when he was home, she felt her authority and independence were compromised, even though she loved him and wanted him to be around.

How *do* you share parenting when you and your mate are not home equally? What if a thorny situation develops that demands an immediate action, and only one of you is available? Although your children will surely benefit from your husband's active involvement in their lives as well as from your willingness to coordinate how you make decisions about them, it's sometimes hard to know when to act on your own and when to check with Dad, and it can be annoying if you feel that you *must* check with him before making any decisions.

Set aside some time to talk with your husband at length about both of your expectations in this regard.

- Try to think through a list of potential parenting issues that might need parental input, and determine which necessitate one-parent and which two-parent permission. For example, whether or not the kids can have a play-date after school is a one-parent job in some families, while a sleepover at a friend's house is a two-parent question. Some couples may prefer that whichever parent is on duty should decide anything unilaterally, while others want even the smallest decisions to be agreed upon by both.

- Set up a major-minor system; either parent can solve minor dilemmas, but major ones require both parents. "Major" would refer to situations in which your child's safety or maturity may be questionable, conflicting interests must be weighed, and choices about which one of you is too ambivalent or uncertain to decide wisely. "Minor" concerns are those that pose no emotional, intellectual, legal, moral, or physical danger or inconvenience to anyone. Major decisions might include whether or not a six year-old may have her ears pierced or if a sixteen year-old should be allowed to go to a coed party, while minor decisions would relate to what to pack in the school lunch.

- Whenever possible, discuss your child's issue when you're together. Brainstorm as a couple or family about what to do to solve the problem.
- If your husband is not physically present, use the phone or email to keep him current on family happenings.
- Make sure that your husband's interest in being a hands-on parent doesn't undermine your authority. Do not pull the "wait until your father gets home" routine, as that puts your husband too firmly in the disciplinarian's role, and makes you appear to be incapable of managing the kids on your own. Make it clear to your children that you each consult the other about big issues, and that either of you acts as the representative of the other on smaller issues.
- When either of you needs to check with the other, do so. Children don't always need answers immediately. Your child can wait until you've had a chance to check in with each other in most circumstances. That also reinforces the idea that the two of you provide a united front.
- Don't let the children play you against each other. If one of you is a "pushover," that parent should know to consult with the other before agreeing to anything.
- Similarly, don't make one or the other of you into the "heavy." Present a united front. If the answer is "no," make sure your child knows that both you and your husband are stating "no" equally. Blaming the other parent ("I'd let you, but Dad won't.") may make you look like a hero, but it damages your marriage and confuses your children.

Talk to your husband about what goes on with the children, and discuss with him your ideas and attitudes about how you are raising them so that whatever you do, your parenting and your husband's are in concert. When you are feeling that your husband's input diminishes yours, tell him. If he feels that you are keeping him at a distance by making parenting decisions without him, include him more frequently. Remember that you had children together because you already admired, loved, and respected each other. Do not allow your need to feel in control make you put each other down; when you work together, your husband participating when he is able, everyone benefits.

Now that we have children, the balance in our marriage seems off; he makes more money than I do, and I am more intimately connected to our children. If we each have areas of strength, why don't I feel like we are equal partners anymore?

Most likely, you feel that the balance is off because it has changed, not because it is unequal. If you and your husband each make valuable contributions to your family, regardless of whether or not those contributions are measurably equal, then your marriage may be more balanced than you realize. Many marriages go through similar transitions when the children are born, and many women worry that they are no longer as powerful or valued in their relationship.

It seems to me that if your husband is willing and able to be the major breadwinner in your family and you enjoy your daily, more intimate involvement with your children, then you have found an excellent balance. Fulfilling different roles in your family does not have to lead to feeling less respect or less importance in the home. All too often, though, we equate monetary income with value, and that may be what makes you feel as if you now have less power in your marriage.

Examine how you and your husband relate to each other now that your roles are so distinctly different. Does your husband assume that he should make most of the decisions about money because you are bringing in less financially? Do you frequently defer to your husband on issues that you could easily be deciding on your own? Do your children seem to respect you less than they respect their dad? Do you feel bad that you are not earning more money? Do you feel less worthy of making any decisions in your family because you aren't contributing financially? If the answers to any of these questions are "yes," someone in your family, maybe even you, isn't adequately valuing your participation in the family.

You may not have an unbalanced marriage, but you may have an unbalanced idea of what it means to be equal partners in a marriage. As long as you both agree that your contributions are equally necessary and supportive of the family goals and ideals, then you have every right to consider your marriage well-balanced. Most partnerships thrive when each party does what he or she does well, complementing rather than duplicating what each does for the other and for the benefit of the family. But many people who believe that women should be able to "do everything" or "have it all" mistakenly think that if the mom in a family isn't working for a salary comparable to her husband's, then she is relinquishing power. I believe that marriage is a partnership, and one in which the participants themselves get to choose how they will balance pleasure, power, and responsibility.

If you feel your husband believes that he should have more control over family decision-making, let him know that it bothers you and explain to him that you see your current division of labor in your family as different than before, but still equally important.

If you struggle to accept the worth of your closeness to your children and your home, spend a few moments calculating what it would cost to hire someone to do all that you do for your family.

Your marriage doesn't need to become unbalanced just because you don't bring in as much cash. You and your entire family need to appreciate *all* of the work necessary to raise children and understand that nurturing a family financially and emotionally are both extremely important. If you and your husband continue to feel that he is now the dominant partner, you may each need to do some soul searching, or perhaps individual or marital therapy, in order to return to a balance that fits you both better.

Both my husband and I feel that our marriage is too much about chores and too little about fun, and we're both exhausted and feel bad. Does it have to be like this?

Of course not. You are the grown-ups in this family; you get to make the rules, and the rules can certainly include a whole lot of fun. Sometimes it's hard to feel comfortable letting things go just to do something frivolous, but fun should be considered as necessary as taking out the trash. You must make fun a priority, and perhaps set the bar a bit lower on how much or how hard you work.

Plan time for fun just as you would schedule doctor's visits or time for homework. Set aside three hours a week, half an hour a day or whatever makes sense for your marriage and your family—just for fun. Set the timer or an alarm clock, if necessary, and when it's time for fun, stop vacuuming, leave the laundry where it is, and do something enjoyable together. Katie and Derek have vowed that after 8:30 PM on Monday and Friday evenings, they do no work of any kind; with the kids in bed, the two of them play board games or cards. Saturday mornings are set aside for fun in Heidi and Justin's family; they take the kids on field trips, play tag, or sometimes rent movies and watch them together in their pajamas. Both families cherish these times, and when it's time to get back to work, whether around the house, for school, or for their jobs, they feel less burdened by all the chores because they've had some fun together.

Be sure also to go out without the kids, if only for a couple of hours, at least once a month. Set aside some time on a regular basis that you will devote to each other. Don't do chores, like grocery shopping, unless you consider that entertainment. Do not include going to the kids' activities, either, even if you enjoy them. Find something that is grown-up and fun to do together.

- Get away from your children overnight, preferably for two or three days at least. You don't have to hire a sitter or even go away, although if you can, that's fabulous, too. For a cheaper approach, swap weekends with another couple whose kids are compatible with yours (they take all of the kids one weekend, you take all of the kids at your house a different weekend), and stay home, sleeping late, eating leisurely, giving each other backrubs, or watching movies together. What's essential is that you spend some extended time alone with your mate, and two or three days is preferable because it takes many loving parents that long to unwind and reconnect as a couple.
- Start a new interest, hobby, or project together. Go for daily walks, or take dance lessons. Take up a new sport or art project, something neither of you has ever done before that you can both enjoy.

At times, drop everything and let chores go. Do something spontaneous and goofy, or just cuddle. Eat ice cream sundaes for lunch, go on a family scavenger hunt, or organize a football or card game on the spur of the moment. Invite your neighbors over. You can include the kids in this one if you do it often enough; just make sure that you take the time to do something fun at least once a week.

Some couples also need to lower their standards. In an effort to be wonderful parents and providers, they lose sight of what is really important as parents and as spouses. As long as there's enough money for food, shelter, and clothing, and your home is clean and tidy enough to be comfortable and safe, you are providing adequately for your family. The greater gift that you can give your children and your marriage than simply those material comforts is the ability to enjoy life. Having fun yourselves not only brings *you* pleasure; it also shows your children that having a good time and finding enjoyment in your relationships and activities is just as important as working. Those are good values to pass along.

Definitely plan to include fun in your lives. Make the conscious effort to set aside the time to devote to hobbies and friends. It is okay to vacuum less often or be less focused on the drudgery of work. Keep fun in your marriage; most couples find that everything gets done eventually, whether or not they take time to have fun together, and having fun makes life much richer.

With a little effort, you and your husband can have a lot of fun despite your busy lives and many responsibilities. Change your dull pattern now. Having an enjoyable marriage is good for you; it provides security and a positive example for your children, and it's a good investment for the future. Having fun as a couple as well as with your family is worth letting the dishes pile up once in a while and will create much better memories of childhood for your kids.

I feel guilty that my husband and I often argue and disagree about parenting issues. How can we work together so that our different attitudes about parenting don't destroy us or our kids?

Good parents come in many styles. Although you and your spouse frequently disagree, you may both be certain that you are right, and that can be very troubling. You can become better parents, though, through open communication, open minds, and some effort on both your parts.

Spend some time talking with your husband about the goals and values you each want to convey to your children, rather than the specifics of each situation. Listen to each other respectfully, and try to understand what your differences are and why. Figure out what each of you cares about most and try to honor that in each other. Come to some consensus about what you consider essential; reach some agreement about what you want your kids to learn about the world and the values you *both* want to pass along. If you agree on these underlying concepts, then how you go about raising your children to reach those goals should become less problematic.

It's okay if you and your husband disagree on the more minor issues, such as whether or not the kids must eat all of their broccoli. Children need to learn to get along with many different people, and knowing that you tolerate rowdier behavior than Dad does, or that Dad needs them to be tidier than Mom does, teaches your kids to be adaptable and considerate of others. But they also need consistency and predictability. So on the big issues, like honesty, you and your husband need to show them that you are in agreement.

Figure out what are your big issues and stick to them. Support each other's approach when the details don't matter, and try to understand why the differences between you continue. If you still cannot find ways to compromise on the small stuff, don't worry. There are many ways to be a great parent, and your children have the advantage of learning from and being loved by two very different parents. Try to keep the general rules consistent and clear. If there is no confusion about what the expectations are, the children will understand.

On the other hand, if you and your husband have fundamentally different ideas about how to raise children, you may need to do some serious work. If your husband believes in spanking and you are vehemently opposed, or if you expect the kids to acquiesce immediately to your demands, no questions asked, while your husband believes that all decisions should be made democratically, then you may have to work harder to find a way to coparent that doesn't create chaos and confusion for the kids.

If you and your husband's basic values and attitudes about raising children actually reflect both techniques and life attitudes that are too different from each other for your continued comfort or for the children's well-being, then counseling might be beneficial. Your kids and your marriage need a minimal amount of agreement and consistency, and if your basic values are too far apart, getting professional support may be wise.

My husband helps me with the baby and housework more than anyone else's husband I know. Why does this make me feel guilty instead of proud or grateful?

Although this may strike some moms as a problem they'd love to have, having the "best" husband around can be stressful, too. Let's face it, even if your husband does more work around the house than any other daddy you know, if he doesn't help the way you want him to, if his constant involvement makes you worry that he thinks you can't manage without him, or if his wonderfulness leads lots of people to rave about how lucky you are while ignoring *your* hard work, that's not all roses. On top of the bad feelings you have, you believe that you *should* feel proud or grateful when, actually, annoyed or jealous describes you better.

Susanne, a working mother of three school-aged children, couldn't understand why she hated how perfect her husband was until her best friend, Cheryl, told her, one too many times, how she wished her own husband did half as much to help with their kids and house. Susanne sheepishly admitted to Cheryl that she was more annoyed than grateful when her husband cooked or cleaned. She didn't like how he folded the clothes or cooked the broccoli, and she hated how everyone made such a fuss over how great he was for doing anything around the house, when no one ever seemed impressed by how much *she* did every very long day.

Once she could articulate these feelings, she realized that her dissatisfaction reflected her lack of self-confidence as a mom and recognized that she needed emotional support as much as or more than practical support. She shared her feelings with both Cheryl and her own husband. Her husband still helps around the house, but in addition, both her husband and her good friend remember to compliment and praise her much more often.

Try to figure out what bothers *you* about being married to Superdad. Most of the time, what's annoying about being married to an extremely helpful and handy man has one of three causes. One, while it may seem impressive, what he does doesn't really help because he does it all "wrong." Two, his doing so much around the house makes you feel that you aren't a good enough mother. And three, people still seem to make a big deal about men who do housework or child care, while taking the efforts of equally hardworking women as a matter of course.

Once you determine what annoys you, you can set things right.

- If you feel that your husband's approach to helping is causing more problems than it solves, you may need to learn to relax your standards. As long as he doesn't do anything dangerous, so what if he puts the cereal bowls in a different cupboard than you would? If you complain or, worse, re-do whatever he does, soon he will stop doing anything around the house. Each of you probably knows how to manage a home reasonably well; doing things differently than each other not only is harmless; it also ultimately teaches your children (and you) flexibility. And if he really botches things up despite honestly wanting to do well, teach him, with respect and affection, what and how you like things done.

- If your husband's efforts make you think that he thinks you are doing a poor job yourself, examine the reality of your lives together. He may actually be so amazed at all you do that he pitches in so that he doesn't feel lazy himself. Or maybe he just loves housework or child care or wants to do more than his own father did. Unless you have evidence, don't allow your own insecurities to lead you to assume that your husband thinks you're a failure. He may feel just as inept at parenting and is working extra hard to prove he can be a good dad.

- ❧ People still assume that "typical" men don't show domestic or nurturing tendencies, so those who do housework or provide child care do receive a disproportionate amount of admiration from outsiders. Try not to resent the adulation directed at Dad; instead, when you witness a similar situation, go out of your way to lavish compliments on the mom who works her job, picks up the baby at day care, and throws a roast in the oven. And tell your friends and family that, as much as you appreciate your husband's phenomenal fatherhood, you're not exactly worthless yourself.

As you know, you are lucky indeed to have a spouse so willing to work hard at home as well as at the office, but it's normal and rational to appreciate all that he does while finding certain aspects of this magnificent man annoying. Just try to understand where your annoyance comes from; minimizing your discomfort will allow you to value him and his contributions more wholeheartedly, and that's good for your whole family.

My husband and I both feel terrible that we seem to have no social life any more. What can we do to resurrect it?

Many couples become so consumed with work and child care that they gradually let their social lives fade away, often not even noticing how long they've gone without seeing anyone from their child-free lives. If you both want to regain some social contacts separate from your children's activities and play dates, you can certainly do so. It just takes a bit of thought and effort.

- Take the first step. Friends from your pre-parenting lives may be thrilled to hear from you. Make the call, send an email, or send a paper invitation, but extend yourselves. Depending on the ages of your children and your finances, you can plan a night out or suggest a potluck meal at your place. If possible, plan an activity that doesn't include the children, unless you know that all the kids will be compatible or that your child-free friends won't mind.
- Meet new people. Join a group or class in an area of interest to you and your mate. Suggest to that friendly neighbor or woman in your exercise class, or to the parents of your son's best friend from preschool, that you and your spouses do something together.
- Do things with other families. Plan an outing to the zoo or invite everyone over to your house. If the kids are reasonably close in age, family friendships can be very satisfying and sometimes last a lifetime.
- Hire a sitter or make plans with an agreeable friend or relative to swap baby-sitting regularly. Once you and your children get accustomed to you and your husband going out, your social life will flourish again.
- Subscribe to a local theater company, the opera, or become museum members. Attend their events. Sign up with another couple and you'll be guaranteed to see them at least a few times a year.
- Become regulars at a local hangout that suits your interests. Many bars, coffee houses, restaurants, community centers, and craft stores host musical guests or activities for the public, often according to particular themes (such as blues clubs, karaoke groups, Asian cooking classes, or needlework

clubs). These often cost relatively little and may introduce you to people with similar tastes and attitudes.

These are just a few ways to boost a sagging social life. Taking that first leap, reaching out to people with whom you've lost touch or to relative strangers, can be scary, but chances are that they will be just as pleased to establish closer ties. Be emotionally courageous, make the effort, and your social life should be back on track in no time.

My husband and I had a great sex life before we had children. I feel really guilty that I'm too tired at the end of each day to even think about sex anymore. How can I bring back that loving feeling?

Regina, the first-time mother of seven-week-old Logan, asked her friend, Maria, the mother of two grown daughters, when she'd felt ready to have sex again after giving birth. Without skipping a beat, Maria replied, "When the kids went to college." While that answer is a bit extreme, many mothers of young children share those feelings. Lots of couples struggle to resume a satisfying sex life once there are children in the home, and many factors may contribute to your decreased interest in sex.

    ➻ Make sure that there are no physical problems that limit your lust. Sometimes hormones do not return to a nonpregnancy state until many months after delivery. Sometimes it's a fear of discomfort or outright pain that decreases your libido. See your health care team to rule out any medical problem that may influence or inhibit your desire.

❧ Many couples with young children just don't get enough sleep. Exhaustion leads many young parents to prefer sleeping to sleeping together. Make sure that you get enough sleep on a regular basis, or at least occasionally, and your interest in lovemaking may increase with your increase in energy.

❧ Often, time seems at such a premium that everything else takes priority over lovemaking. Try to make sure that you and your husband go to bed at the same time. If one of you consistently falls asleep before the other, lovemaking becomes less likely, so don't let that happen. Develop a marital bedtime ritual that includes a goodnight hug and kiss, and some conversation and cuddling, and your interest in each other might be piqued again.

❧ Some women feel that they just aren't as attractive as they were in their pre-parenthood days, and so resist caresses that may make their love handles or stretch marks more noticeable. Talk to your husband because he probably couldn't care less how you look. Knowing he loves you just as you are may help spark that loving feeling again.

❧ Many mothers feel that they spend all of every day giving to their kids, their husbands, their friends, their extended families, and to their jobs. They often describe having sex as just one more thing they must do for someone else, forgetting that lovemaking should be satisfying for both parties. Make a conscious effort to remember that you used to enjoy being intimate with your mate, and that it should be enjoyable once again.

❧ Some mothers feel that their husbands work such long hours that they hardly see each other anymore. Women often want to spend some time connecting emotionally before they are interested in connecting physically. If your husband is too consumed with work, find uninterrupted time together at least once a week or once a month to talk and reconnect in all ways. Listen to each other, share thoughts, a meal, and a back rub, light some candles, put on some music, and get to know each other again.

- Occasionally, especially for mothers of young children, it's hard to make the mental switch from being a mom to being a lover. You need to accept and become comfortable with the idea that mothers are whole people, fully capable of loving a child as well as being a loving sexual partner. Sexuality is an important part of a loving relationship, and it's completely okay for you to be a wonderful mom and still have an active sex life.

- Knowing that your children are in the next room puts a damper on many couple's sexual fires because they worry that the kids will overhear or somehow just *know* what's going on between Mommy and Daddy. Many loving couples have learned to be extremely quiet when they make love; some make love early in the morning when they know that their children will sleep through anything, or only when the kids are not home so that they can feel free enough to fully engage in lovemaking. Being a bit more creative and quiet might be all you need.

- It's good for you, as well as for your children, that you and your husband have a loving and intimate relationship. (Of course, please don't tell your children about your love life. They really don't want to know about your sex life; they will benefit simply from seeing that you love each other. It's just that when you are sexually intimate, that closeness usually spills over into how you treat each other, and witnessing that closeness generally reassures the children of your love for each other.)

Take the time to figure out what prevents you and your husband from resuming the intimacy you once enjoyed and you should be able to regain it. Many, many couples have experienced diminished interest in each other sexually and still managed to find their way back. It's good for you as well as for your children for you and your husband to have a loving and intimate relationship—they will benefit simply from seeing that you love each other. They will feel secure when they know that your marriage is secure, and one aspect of a successful marriage is a satisfying love life.

My husband complains that I don't think of him as a person anymore; he thinks I just need him to earn money and help with the kids. What if he's right?

When your kids are young, child care can seem overwhelming. Little kids need lots of attention and parenting requires tremendous energy. While it may sometimes seem to both you and your husband that you value him only for his contributions to keeping the family financially afloat or giving you a break from the kids, you still have some fondness for him beyond his bankrolling or parenting. You may, however, be too tired or overwhelmed to remember what made you love him.

Just as you need support and loving attention in order for your husband to be able to give fully to your children and to you, he must feel appreciated. Please do your husband and yourself a favor and try to remember what brought you two together before you had those lovely youngsters. Too often, parents become so consumed by their responsibilities that they forget to have fun together, or they don't take time to be people as well as parents. Remember that your husband is a grown-up; you love each other, and that is why you chose to make your life together.

Here are a few tips to help you regain a more loving and respectful relationship.

- If child care or work responsibilities exhaust you, get some help or change your schedule.
- Treat your husband lovingly and recognize that he's as overwhelmed by his life as you are with yours.
- Arrange for time to be together as a couple, with no children.
- Listen to how he's spent his day. Really, truly listen.
- Don't try to compete with him over who's had the harder day. Accept that you *each* work very hard to make a good life for your family, and that you each deserve support and respect.
- Be kind to him; compliment how he looks and what he does.
- Say thank you when he helps you, even if you believe he's just doing his job.
- If he is at work and you are not, give him time to unwind and change clothes when he gets home from work before thrusting a crabby child in his face.
- Tell your husband the good things that happen in your day first; don't dwell on the bad.

Being a loving wife will help your husband be a loving husband and vice versa. Although many wives want their husbands to start being the more loving one, someone needs to turn these behaviors around; it might as well be you. When you begin to be nicer, he will be nicer, and you may start remembering what you liked about him so much in the first place. Sharing the joys as well as the burdens of family life will make your conversations more enjoyable and brighten both of your outlooks. Showing that you appreciate him for more than his financial and child-care support will enrich your marriage and provide an excellent example for your children. And being good to each other will help you remember why you chose to go through life together in the first place.

My husband misses how I used to care for him. I feel guilty that he is neglected, but what can I do when I feel too "nurtured out" myself?

Some women do not realize how often they are the giver in their lives until they have children. Before kids, you may have been a fabulous listener, always interested in the social exploits of your best friends. Or maybe you were one of those workaholics, a worker who gave everything to her job and then some. Maybe you expected that once you became a mother, you would still work as hard to be a good friend, spouse, daughter, and worker while also making your home gorgeous, cooking fantastic meals, and helping the kids with homework. If you weren't exhausted from all that giving before, mothering can put you over the edge. When you give everyone else everything you have, there's nothing left over for you and your husband.

Tell your husband! It seems obvious to most moms, but often husbands really don't know how much of their wives' days focuses on taking care of others. I hear this all the time, as mothers take care of the home, the kids, their jobs, their aging relatives, and their friends. Often there is just nothing remaining to give to your husband at the end of each day. Believing that your husband and your marriage can handle what amounts to neglect, you put you and your husband last and no longer nurture your relationship.

So tell your husband when you feel all used up. Explain that you spent the day listening to the woes of your sister-in-law or solving a major problem at work. Share with him how many emails you answered, diapers you changed, carpools you drove, reports you filed, or calls you made about your mother's doctor bills. Tell him you feel all "nurtured out," and assure him that you love him, but feel depleted.

In addition to trying to make sure your husband understands the nature of your daily nurturing activities, you may also need to make some adjustments. If you feel "nurtured out" most of the time, something is out of balance. Either you are doing too much, expecting too much of yourself, or your husband or others are expecting too much of you. Get help, either at work or at home, or limit or eliminate some of your more draining activities or relationships.

Also, take care of yourself. You deserve to have some discretionary emotional giving and to be nurtured yourself. Start to examine which friendships still give you pleasure and which ones seem too demanding. Reconsider your priorities. I would never suggest that you do less than a good job at whatever you undertake, but you might be working so hard to fill everyone else's needs that you have put your own and your husband's needs aside. By reassessing what you honestly value, what gives you satisfaction and what has become an unnecessary chore, you have the opportunity to make better choices and free up some of that emotional energy. When you nurture people and projects you genuinely care about, you will not feel so overextended and you will be able to focus, at least occasionally, on your husband as well.

And if you are neglecting your husband mostly because you are feeling so emotionally overdrawn, taking care of yourself will take care of him—and you will both feel better.

Sometimes I hear myself talking to my husband in a tone of voice I hate; I sound like I'm his not-very-respectful mother. How can I stop treating him like one of the kids?

Oddly, I hear this with some frequency. Callie notices that when she's especially tired or feeling overwhelmed, she bosses her husband around and tells him what to do in a voice she is shocked to discover coming from her own mouth. I think many moms become tired and cranky by the end of the day, and so immersed in running the home that they aren't able to share responsibilities with their husbands. Instead, they mentally lump their husbands into the same category as their children: people they love but over whom they are in charge.

There are two things you can do. First, consciously make an effort to speak kindly and with more patience in general. Many women become rather too comfortable with their families. They forget that even loved ones, maybe especially loved ones, want to be treated kindly and respectfully. If you are in the habit of barking out orders to your children, you may inadvertently speak similarly to your husband. Both your kids and your mate should be treated well; ask them politely to take out the trash or put the milk away, and use a calm voice when making suggestions. When you hear that bossy edge creeping back into your communications, catch yourself. If need be, take a deep breath, leave the room, or grab a cup of tea—but stop, mid-sentence, if necessary, think about what you want to convey, and then say what you want, nicely.

If you are tough only on your husband, and not on your kids, this may be an indication that there are marital issues to work out between you. Maybe you feel that you are shouldering too much of the family burden, maybe you feel that you and your spouse aren't in agreement about priorities or child rearing, or maybe you are just burnt out and dumping your bad feelings on your husband. Be honest with yourself about what you are feeling. Often we behave badly toward those we love most because we feel secure in that love, but treating loved ones badly will be tolerated only so long.

Assess how you are enjoying your life and your marriage. Don't continue to treat your husband as a disobedient child; find out what the real problem is and try to solve what's really bothering you. And do your best to be nice to the people you love. Even if their love for you is guaranteed, it's still more pleasant to be kind to them. In return, they'll be pleasant and no one's feelings need be hurt.

My husband and I argue all the time. Am I right to worry that this can't be good for the kids?

Arguing in front of the children all the time isn't good for the kids or for you. If you and your husband are so at odds that you feel that you are constantly snapping at each other, please do yourselves and your kids a favor and seek professional help right away. With rare exceptions, continuous clashing is bad for your marriage and for your children. Children want their parents to love them and to love each other, and they equate unvarying fighting and arguing with lack of love.

An occasional argument, though, is a different story. Busy and involved people are bound to have disagreements once in a while, or say or do something that might hurt a loved one's feelings—

and arguing may result. Allowing an older child to see that Mommy and Daddy can argue, air their hurt feelings, apologize, and resolve problems can be a very useful practice, as long as it is infrequent and truly does resolve in deeper understanding and acceptance of each other. It can be very instructive for a child to learn that even adults may disagree or hurt each other's feelings, that even adults need to settle disagreements honestly and fairly, and that you can truly love someone and still disagree with them. If you argue graciously, kindly, and somewhat rarely, having an argument in front of the kids should be no problem.

However, just because you argue well doesn't mean you should invite your children in to witness an argument or not worry when an argument begins while the kids are around. Children can find arguing frightening. Parents are entitled to some privacy, and certain aspects of their relationship are truly not the children's business. Sometimes the subject of the argument may be as inappropriate for the kids to witness as the intense and negative emotions surrounding it.

I believe that you should shield the children from the following:

- Children should not hear you or your husband call each other derogatory names or speak negatively about each other's characters.
- They should also not hear you insult or criticize other people, such as other family members or friends.
- Children should not hear threats that one of you will leave the family if some behavior doesn't change.
- Children should not hear threats of violence or withdrawal of financial support.
- Children should definitely not see any physical fighting between parents. The moment an argument turns physical,

you have an extremely serious problem that needs to be dealt with immediately; no one should stay in a marriage with physical violence, and children are particularly at risk in those marriages.

When a disagreement between you and your husband turns harsh, try to keep it out of earshot of your children. Wait until they go to bed or are out of the house (which has the added bonus of allowing you each time to think about the conflict and resolve it more calmly later on) and then resume the argument in hushed voices.

If you are not capable of resolving arguments without a good deal of emotional pain, seek professional assistance. Many relationships go through periods when the couple feels out of touch with each other, but couples who can't handle disagreements without a lot of noisy arguing or who argue all the time need some help. Constant verbal conflicts aren't good for anyone; you deserve to find better ways to get along with your mate, and your kids deserve to live without the stress of frequently raised and unkind voices. Get help.

My husband and I are discussing divorce. I feel guilty about all the anger and tension in the house. How and what do we tell the kids?

If there is a lot of tension in your marriage, your kids already know. You can talk with them about the fact that Mommy and Daddy are having some trouble getting along, but that you are trying to do better. You can also make a point to avoid screaming matches or viciousness in their presence.

If your marriage is shaky, or if divorce is actually imminent, then be honest but kind.

- ❧ Do not share the details of any wrongdoing of either you or your husband. Particularly if there has been any cheating, abuse, or dishonesty, as tempting as it may be to dump the blame on your soon-to-be-ex.
- ❧ Reassure the children that they will be well taken care of, regardless of what happens to your marriage.
- ❧ Reassure your children that they have absolutely nothing to do with the problems between you and their father. If you argue about the kids, make doubly sure that they know that you argue because you don't see things similarly, not because there's anything wrong about the kids.
- ❧ If a divorce is imminent, share facts with the children.
- ❧ Do not ask your children to take sides, to choose one parent over the other.
- ❧ Do not use your children as intermediaries. If you need to take something to your mate, do it and leave the kids out. If things are really nasty, use a relative or attorney to act as the bridge between you.
- ❧ Do not use your children as spies, asking them to tell you what daddy does when they're with him, or pumping them for information about their other parent.
- ❧ Don't treat your children as if they are now adults. Do not rely on them to fill in for the unavailable parent. Let them be kids. Do not give them responsibilities that are based on your needs (that they learn to cook at age six) rather than on their needs.
- ❧ Do not start bribing your children or overindulging them because you feel guilty about your marriage falling apart.

⊛ Be a grown-up about this. As difficult as this is on you, it is also difficult on your children.

Be as honest as you can be without being hurtful. Give a few details and be loving and mature with your children. Get help if you or the kids need it. Divorce is hard on the whole family, even when it is the best solution. Do what you need for yourself, but bear in mind that your children still need you, that their father is just as much a part of them as you are.

I'm beginning to think that my husband would rather be at work than at home. I'd feel terrible if that were true, so how can I make him want to be home more?

Many working dads *and* moms occasionally prefer being at work to being at home. Work is predictable, clean, and there is no crying. You get lunch breaks, no one pulls on your clothes or yells in your ear when you make telephone calls, and you're among grown-ups with similar interests and talents. Your assignments are usually clearly defined, you are good at what you do, and when you finish, you get paid for your efforts. It sounds pretty appealing.

If your husband really would rather be at work than at home, find out what aspects of family life he's trying to avoid. Many husbands feel that they spend the day working very hard so that their families can have every economic advantage, and then the minute they get home they are expected to take care of the kids or do household chores, often without any time to change their clothes or take a break. If they don't pitch in right away, their wives get testy or berate them for being inconsiderate, their kids demand their attention, and they feel belittled, undervalued, or guilty. No wonder they prefer to stay at work.

Although it may be reasonable and socially acceptable for men to be nurturing and helpful when they are at home, after they have worked long hours, many dads feel they need and deserve a break. Of course, their wives have worked long hours, too, and feel the same need for respite. The problem isn't that work is so much more attractive than home; the problem is that no one gets enough time to take care of his or her own needs.

If home is to be as appealing as work, then being at home needs to feel more relaxing, welcoming, and loving, and less like unpaid, unskilled, and underappreciated work.

Make a conscious effort to treat each other well. Change the coming-home experience to something that you each look forward to; greet your husband lovingly and allow him time to make the emotional transition from worker to husband before you start asking him for support. If you are always home before he is, handle the dinner preparation tasks while he unwinds, and then ask him to be in charge of clean up. Be appreciative of all that *each* of you does to keep your family afloat. Value equally each person's financial, housekeeping, and child-care contributions to the family well-being.

In addition, if your husband does help around the house, do not criticize him! Work may become more attractive than home if he is always made to feel less competent than you, or if he feels that you are in charge, and he is your assistant in housekeeping or child care. If you want your husband's active involvement in the home, you must treat his methods and efforts with respect. Any man who feels respected and valued at work would be insane to look forward to being at home if he feels incompetent or taken for granted by the people who should love him best. Everyone wants to feel good about what they do and everyone wants to feel appreciated. If your husband feels unappreciated or incompetent at home, work will naturally feel more attractive to him.

If you work all day, make sure that both you and your husband strive to foster a peaceful place for your children to come home to. If you want your husband to look forward to returning to you and your kids at the end of every day, make your home a welcoming, loving place. I'm not asking you to be a submissive wife here; rather, I am suggesting that you treat each other well and that you create an inviting and warm home atmosphere. Remember, being respectful, supportive, and grateful to your husband models polite and loving behavior to your children, makes your husband feel good, motivates him to be more involved with the family, and ultimately, makes him appreciate you more, too. That's the way to guarantee that home is a place where all family members want to be.

I'm starting to resent it that my husband leaves all the planning and arrangements for family activities to me. How can I get him more involved?

Despite great strides toward equality between the sexes, when the family includes both a husband and a wife, stereotypical gender roles often influence who does what around the house. Old habits and expectations are hard to break, and typically, it has always been the wife who organizes the family social life. You may resent his lack of involvement, but it's quite possible that your husband doesn't even know that this is an issue for you.

Try approaching this directly. Mention to your husband that you've noticed that he seems to leave all the planning for family activities to you and propose that it might be nice to share that responsibility occasionally. Tell him that you want his input as well as his help so that planning for the family is more fun for you all.

- ❧ Designate certain weekends, events, or activities for which each of you will be responsible.
- ❧ If friends call to make a date, ask him to be the one to plan a get-together.
- ❧ Keep a family calendar in a prominent place in your home on which you and your husband record all planned activities. He will know without asking you what days are free and can add to it himself.
- ❧ Whoever is the closer friend or relative of the people with whom you are socializing could be designated to be the one to make the call. If you are going to visit his sister, for example, then he gets to do the planning.
- ❧ Or do the opposite—he sets up plans with your friends and relatives, you with his—so that you each get to know these friends and extended family members better.
- ❧ Take turns making plans, such as trips to the botanical gardens, apple picking, or bowling, for your immediate family. Outings for just your family create wonderful shared memories.
- ❧ You and your husband could each have designated and specific jobs. For instance, he might always be the one to arrange for a sitter, or to be in charge of the violin lessons and monitoring the practicing. Divide the jobs up according to interest and availability so that each of you is readily capable of maintaining control over your specific family domain.
- ❧ Alternatively, plan everything together. Consulting with each other before confirming any dates or activities or buying tickets keeps both of you involved.

If getting your husband to take charge of more family activities still eludes you, you may have to handle it in a less constructive fashion. Some women find that even after discussing and planning to share these responsibilities fairly, their husbands refuse to cooperate, or they agree to be more involved yet don't follow through. In these cases, you must decide how strongly you feel he should participate in the social planning. If you think it is essential that he takes a part in some of the activity planning, once you've agreed on who is in charge of what, you must not do what he's agreed to do. If he now has social responsibilities at home and they don't get done—well then, they don't. If you decide that you will no longer make plans to visit his parents or invite his parents over, for example, then you must do nothing to arrange to see them until your husband takes care of it. When several weeks or more go by without your customary trip to Grandma and Grandpa's house, he might start to notice.

If things do not improve, you may need to accept that he is simply not interested in assisting you in the family activity planning. If your resentment seems to be getting out of control, consider what else your husband does to support you around the house. You may need to talk with him about your feelings and shift some other responsibilities so you don't feel so overburdened. Ideally, you will both enjoy many of the things you do for your family and feel that each of you contributes fairly. Remember that you each make unique contributions to your family, and that not everything needs to be perfectly even and equal for it to be fair. And when both of you feel that things are fair, you won't resent it if they're not exactly equal.

Chapter Four

Motherhood and Family

What Danielle wanted more than anything was to be a loving and competent wife and mother, a warm and giving friend, an affectionate and generous family member, and a fabulous worker. When Danielle had her second child, she had a complicated delivery and difficult recovery, so her mother-in-law came to help. She stayed in Danielle's home and cooked, cleaned, and did the laundry. Danielle worked hard to take care of the kids, get enough rest, check in at her office, and try to keep the house functioning. She knew she couldn't have managed it without her mother-in-law's support, and she really appreciated how hard her mother-in-law worked to help the family function.

What she didn't appreciate was the constant barrage of "suggestions" as to how she might do everything better. Her mother-in-law criticized everything, from how the towels were folded to the way she carried her son. Danielle tried to get her husband to intervene, but he wanted no part of their clashes. He enjoyed having his mother around, and the last thing he wanted was to be put in the middle of the two women he loved best. Danielle, with a lot of determination, was able to keep her annoyance and hurt feelings under control, though, as she so greatly needed the help.

Until one morning. Danielle woke up early with the baby and, hungry herself, went to the kitchen to make some toast. She couldn't find her toaster. Her mother-in-law had taken it upon herself to rearrange the entire kitchen. She had moved all the small appliances, reorganized the contents of all the cabinets, replaced her kitchen towels, alphabetized her spices, and tossed out half the contents of her freezer! Danielle was fuming. She didn't know how she was going to manage it politely, but she needed to find a way to stay in her mother-in-law's good graces while setting clearer boundaries and limits on what was acceptable (and what was not) for her mother-in-law to do. If her mother-in-law didn't start behaving more respectfully of Danielle's feelings and home, Danielle was sure that World War Three would break out in her living room.

I've heard many stories about intrusive mothers-in-law, and more than one story like Danielle's. I've been told about mothers-in-law who go into their adult sons' drawers and throw out and replace the worn out underwear, mothers-in-laws who move all the furniture in their son and daughter-in-law's homes, and mothers-in-law who insist that their daughters-in-law wait on them hand and foot, even when the daughter-in-law has a new baby to take care of. Those mother-in-law jokes continue for good reason. Fathers may threaten to kill anyone who might hurt their precious baby girls, but mothers have their own tactics for dealing with the women who come between them and their sons. There appears to be a special bond between mothers and sons, and therefore a special stress on the relationship between that same mother and the woman who usurps her role as the most important woman in her son's life.

Fortunately, I also hear about wonderfully close relationships within extended families. In-laws can also become close friends and confidants. When couples have children together, those children create bonds that extend beyond the walls of their own home. The kids provide a biological connection between mothers-in-law, daughters-in-law, sons-in-law and fathers-in-law, and between siblings and their children. Even if you had nothing in common before, children can bring you all together. Sometimes, whether you want them to or not.

While having an interest in your children can forge warm bonds among you and your relatives, other issues often arise as well. How to spend holidays, competition among grandparents for the affection and attentions of the grandchildren, competition between adult siblings or siblings-in-law about the accomplishments of their respective children, and squabbles about how best to raise children may develop even among the most civilized and loving family members. Things as simple as who gets to bring the eggnog, or as complicated as how to deal with family crises, create tension when there are two or more coping or personality styles, expectations, and attitudes involved. When there's a divorce in the family, relationships become even more complicated; loyalties are tested and formerly close ties are severed.

This chapter faces the many concerns that cause mothers to feel guilty about their interactions with family members. Many mothers feel that it is their duty to make sure that everybody they care about feels good, and sometimes that is a harder job than it seems. One child needs one thing, your husband needs another, and you don't know which way to turn first. Mothers place tremendous demands on themselves, and when a mother expects herself to do everything for everybody in her family, she inevitably disappoints herself—and sometimes her loved ones.

This chapter helps a mother recognize when she and her family are being unrealistic in their expectations of her and helps her juggle everyone's needs, including her own.

We mothers also become fiercely protective of our children and ourselves when we sense danger. Although children give you something incomparable to share with your extended family, the increased contact and interest can bring with it increased irritations. Mothers need to be honest about their feelings, protect themselves and their children when they feel under fire or overwhelmed, and also find ways to be polite, loving, and respectful. This chapter also suggests ways to be close to your relatives without placing blame, and without making yourself or them too crazy.

I think having relatives around is wonderful for kids. No one besides you and your husband will care for your children and you as much as your parents or other relatives will. No one else will care as much about the triumphs and tragedies that befall your immediate family. Ideally you will forge strong and positive relationships with all extended family members.

What's sometimes tricky is to be able to have both sides of the family around when you want and need them, to have privacy when you need that, and to have loving and supportive emotions in all directions. No one should feel that anyone else is too intrusive or critical; everyone should feel respected. You want to develop cordial relationships with your mate's family as well as your own and find ways to blend or manage the various personalities and attitudes so that feelings are not hurt. For many families, this balance is a challenge to maintain, and it's a balance that changes as you become more confident in your parenting skills, your children's needs change, or your work demands shift.

Ideally, you will develop ways to remain close to your extended families. Ideally, you will become adept at managing differences in family celebration styles, conflict resolution, and competitive issues. We all need all the warmth and nurturing we can get, and we all need very little in the way of harsh or unsupportive criticism. Families can provide superior nurturing, and when you're raising young children, having supportive relatives nearby can be a blessing.

The contents of this chapter focus on the less than ideal, though, because as wonderful and positive as families can be, they can also be the source of frequent tensions, hurt feelings, and mis-understandings. As much as you adore your mother, for example, she can also drive you nuts. Your husband may be very close to his brother, but you may think he's a real jerk. And no matter how much you may bad mouth your own blood ties, if your husband says the same unkind thing about one of your relatives that you said just last week, you're likely to want to deck him. Managing life with your extended family takes effort, consideration, patience, understanding, and maturity. When you're in the midst of raising a family, you may need some guidance to help you regain your clear-headed and loving family balance. This chapter should help you deal with family members.

How can I keep up with all the demands and needs of each family member?

Women agonize over how much is expected of them, and often feel that they never catch up, running from one responsibility to another. Sometimes the demands seem so overwhelming that we don't even stop to consider whether or not they are reasonable. Many times, moms do things for family members who could just as easily take care of themselves, and sometimes, when a woman feels pulled in so many different directions, her emotional state makes her less efficient. To combat that feeling of being a human tug-of-war rope, you need know what your priorities are and learn to focus. First of all, figure out if you should even be doing all that your various family members ask of you. Second, once you've decided to take something on, focus on the job at hand and accept that you can only be one place at a time.

Dorothy, a woman who married young and at one time had three children under the age of seven, told me that it took her a long time to realize that she didn't always have to do something just because someone wanted or expected her to, nor did she need to do it immediately. For years she felt that she was disappointing others by not taking care of everything rapidly or well enough (by her own standards). But then, one winter, she came down with pneumonia. Lo and behold, despite her inability to care for her family, life went on; her husband and kids managed just fine while she recuperated in bed for days on end. When she was fully recovered, she decided that each family member was more capable than she'd ever given them credit for and that she would be glad to do what was necessary, but no longer was she going to do for others what they could do for themselves.

Sue, a professor, had two little girls who seemed to require a lot of attention. She had no trouble figuring out what jobs she needed to be doing and was very good about assigning her children specific, age-appropriate chores. But she found herself constantly distracted, thinking about cooking dinner while she was folding laundry and feeling as if she'd abandoned her first child if she was singing and dancing with her baby. Talking with a friend about how guilty she felt no matter what she was doing helped her see that she was keeping up very well; she just wished she could be in two places at once. Recognizing the futility of that wish, she began to let herself off the hook a bit. Now, when she's helping her older one with homework, if the younger tries to distract her, she reminds her that her turn is coming. She is calmer about what she is doing for whom and when and no longer feels guilty because she knows that she is doing enough for everyone.

Make an honest assessment of what needs to be done. If you are doing more than you should, teach your children to pitch in more often. Consider who may be capable of getting which things done and who should be responsible for doing them, and start assigning chores. Don't do things for your family members when they could be doing them themselves.

Learn to distinguish between needs and wants. Figure out what tasks need immediate attention and what can wait. Sometimes mothers feel overwhelmed because they believe they should be doing whatever is asked of them. Instead, consider each request individually. Don't say "yes" or "no" without considering whether you are the best or only person to fulfill the need. When you decide to take care of something, stay focused on the task at hand.

Finally, remind yourself how much you do for everyone. Just because you can't always do everything for everyone that you, or they, might want you to doesn't mean that you aren't highly competent and efficient. You may just be trying to do more than makes sense. And don't forget to be kind to yourself as well; if you don't take care of your own needs, you will burn out, be resentful, or exhaust yourself, and then you won't be of much value to anyone.

How can I make sure that everyone gets a fair share of my time and attention?

Maybe you need to think about what it means to be fair. If you believe that everyone in your family should have equal and unlimited access to your full attention, you will find it very difficult indeed to try to take care of everyone fairly. Everyone else's needs will seem endless and there will be no time to take care of yourself. Family members are likely to recognize that you feel it is your duty to cater to them, and they will demand your services accordingly, regardless of the other family members' needs, abilities, or skills. If every member of your family believes that you are there to take care of him or her, they will expect you to do just that, and they will be disappointed when you don't.

Some moms feel very bad if they have to spend noticeably more time with one family member than another. But real life is like that sometimes. As you all grow up and mature, children will become more independent. Over the course of time, each person in the family is likely to be needy for certain periods and carefree for others. Instead of worrying about dividing your attention equally, think about filling the most important needs. Your kids and husband will feel that you treat them fairly when they feel that you are responsive to their needs; if they know you love them and are there for them, if each person you love feels they have enough of your time and attention, they won't care or even notice how much actual time you spend with each of them.

It sounds like you may be so worried about taking care of everyone fairly that you have inadvertently conveyed to your family that you are not emotionally available. If instead of keeping track of how much time you devote to each family member, you maintain the attitude that you are there to help them when they truly need your assistance, and to offer support and guidance so that they may become independent whenever possible, your husband and kids will all feel that you are a giving and fair mom.

How can I know when to care for my child and when to care for myself—when we are both needy?

As Amy, a mother and teacher, put it, "There are days when I feel that I have a terrible choice: cranky child or crazy mom." Under the best of circumstances, caring for your children while trying to live your own life is not always easy. You may want some quiet time just when your toddler needs to test his legs and lungs. Your work may require your full attention exactly when your daughter wants help on a school project. Family life often seems to present moms with conflicting demands. Most of the time, it isn't too hard to know what can wait and what can't. You take care of the more pressing situation first or delegate tasks to family members who are more available. But sometimes you may feel that you cannot respond to your child appropriately, and then it is time for you to take a break.

When you feel that if you have to read one more story you will start to scream, or when your child asks for a treat and you want to run away, you know that you must take care of yourself so that you will be able to take care of your family. You don't want to be so involved with meeting others' needs that you forget your own. If you neglect yourself, you run the risk of ultimately neglecting others.

Ideally, you should be able to recognize that you are running on empty, and when you are, take care of yourself. Ask yourself these questions:

- Do you often forget to eat or go to the bathroom when you are taking care of your kids?
- Do you find yourself yelling at your kids or husband excessively, or out of proportion to the situation?
- Does your own anger surprise you, or come out suddenly, when you don't expect it?

❧ Do you worry that you will resort to physical force or violence when your kids start nagging at you?

If you have reached the point where your answer to any of the above questions is "yes," then you know you must choose becoming a sane mom over placating your cranky child—or you will both be miserable. And in choosing to be a sane mother, you are also choosing to be able to be a good mother.

When you feel overextended, it's time to make a change. If you are home, trying to get some work done while your child keeps tugging at your sleeve, take a break. Sometimes giving your child just a few minutes of undivided attention may soothe her enough so that she is able to play on her own for a little bit longer, letting you finish your task. If your child just doesn't want to cooperate with whatever you have in mind, switch gears. Remove her from whatever she was doing and go for a walk, put on some dance music, or make some changes in the atmosphere. If your patience has just evaporated, call a friend. See if you can drop your child off for an hour (or ten minutes!) so that you have time to regain your composure, or invite a friend over for your child.

It's fine to take care of yourself first, sometimes. Just be sure that your child is safe and give yourself a break. Truly, taking care of yourself is important.

How can I find time to spend with each family member one-on-one?

With free time at a premium and multiple needs to fill, finding the time to be alone with each family member can feel like one more impossible goal. Of course, it's sometimes difficult to achieve, but it can be done, even with multiple children in the home. Consider what you want your one-on-one time to mean to each of you, and try these ideas.

- First, recognize that time alone together doesn't have to be all that long. Young children have short attention spans, and older children, while they still value time with Mom, have lots of other interests. Aim for ten to twenty minutes of focused, undivided attention on your child or husband and if you sustain it for longer, that's just a bonus.
- Create a family ritual. Maybe you are the bedtime reader for each child while your husband is the nightly bath manager. While Dad is helping Zack scrub behind his ears, you are reading to David. Switch kids so you get to read to Zack while David splashes Dad, and you've each had time alone with each child.
- When driving with younger children, turn off the radio and cell phone. Ask about your child's day and really listen to his or her answer, or sing his or her favorite songs together. Instead of making carpooling or commuting a chore, it can be time for focused conversation or fun.
- Mothers of older children know that sometimes car time is the best time to talk with your child. Preteens and even teens who still need rides to their various events appreciate that you're supporting their interests. And sometimes the lack of eye contact and the absence of the distractions of the phone or TV allow a generally uncommunicative teen to open up.
- If time is truly at a minimum, or if the kids in the family outnumber the adults, take turns spending time one-on-one,

and consider a weekly (or even monthly) rather than daily private dates rather than daily ones. Josh and Leah scheduled weekends for solo time. Each week, Leah would spend Saturday morning with one of their three kids while Josh would take care of the other two, alternating which child got the time alone with Mom. Josh got Sunday mornings for one-on-one contact with one child while Leah took the other two. This way each child had alone time with each parent every three weeks. While creating this system took some effort, the whole family enjoyed the different combinations of who spent time with whom.

- Don't worry that the individual attention needs to be spectacular. Taking just one child on an errand or for a walk in the neighborhood can be plenty. Remember that the goal is not the activity but to be with your child.

- When you are alone with your child, truly be there with him. Ask about his ideas, feelings, and desires, and listen to what he says. Don't judge or try to get other things done while you're supposed to be with him. If that means shortening your time together, that's preferable to pretending to be with your child when you're really mentally somewhere else.

Try to remember that your goal is to have good times with your children and your husband, to connect on an emotional level, and to build good relationships and fond memories. When you are with your loved one, put aside other projects. It is the quality of the emotional interaction that will stay in your hearts and minds, not how much time or money was spent.

My house is a mess and I can't seem to get it together to make a decent meal. Am I a bad mother?

Somehow we seem to think that being a good wife and mother means that you have to be a great housekeeper, nutritionist, and chef. We see TV moms hold down jobs, look gorgeous and sexy, and maintain immaculate homes, or we remember our own mothers managing the home and the children without a fuss. What we don't seem to realize is that TV moms aren't real, and our own mothers probably didn't do everything as effortlessly as it seemed. Nor do we give ourselves enough credit for what we do.

You undoubtedly already take care of the most important aspects of mothering. If you love your children and your husband, provide responsible supervision, safe shelter, adequate nourishment, and consistently meet their physical and emotional needs, aren't you being a great mom? As long as your home is not messy enough to warrant a visit from the police or health department, clutter doesn't make you a bad mother.

There are only so many hours in a day, and being a fabulous mother or wife doesn't necessarily involve excellence in mopping or marinating. You get to choose how to spend your time and talents, and you also have to come to terms with your abilities and limitations. If your mother or sister-in-law runs a spotless home, good for her; if your best friend cooks and decorates magnificently, that's lovely. Other people's achievements don't detract from yours, nor does a perfectly well-run home indicate excellence in motherhood. And by accepting your strengths as well as your weaknesses, you allow your children to accept theirs.

If you want a cleaner home or fancier meals, you could try lots of tricks to get there. You could hire a housekeeper, ask friends to swap services (you help them clean out their closets and they help you weed the garden), or learn to be more efficient. There are cooking classes and books on time and household management to help you become better organized. But at the end of the day, you want to feel good about your relationships and your skills. Don't confuse good mothering with good housekeeping—improve your homemaking skills if you want to, but don't worry that your housekeeping or culinary skills reflect badly (or well!) on your motherhood.

I don't love my husband's nieces and nephews as much as my blood relatives. Should I feel so guilty about this?

Blood sometimes truly is thicker than water. Many adults, if they are honest with themselves, have somewhat different feelings for their biological relatives than for their relatives by marriage. Watching your "baby" sister's daughter dance and sing just like she did when you were both little just strikes a chord that nothing else can match. It doesn't mean that you are a bad person, or that you don't love your husband's relatives; it just means that there is a special place in your heart for those with whom you share some genetic material. As long as you treat the relatives similarly, particularly when in their presence, your more intense feelings for those to whom you are biologically related won't cause problems.

Becca had many nieces and nephews on both sides. She noticed that she felt an automatic connection to her brothers' kids, but needed to get to know her husband's sister's children before she could warm up to them. Elana and her husband lived very near to his brother and sister and their families, and so she was actually much closer to those nieces and nephews than to her own. This set up worked in her favor, though, because she felt that she had very strong attachments to the nieces and nephews she saw regularly, as she was able to share holidays and birthdays with them. Her biological relatives lived a great distance away, but she enjoyed an emotional, more primal connection to them even though she didn't actually know them as well.

As long as you act warmly and lovingly toward all these children (and if you don't give more lavish gifts to one side or another), any differences in your feelings should be minimal and unimportant. Do not let your preferences be discussed and do not play favorites. Think about the love you have for your own brother's and sister's kids as special, not necessarily as more or better. Your relationships with all of the kids can be loving, interested, and warm—and that is good enough.

My husband's family doesn't accept me as a real family member. How can I stop feeling so angry and hurt?

Families are kind of funny about boundaries; some families generously include all new family members, whether joining the family by marriage or birth, while others keep those newcomers at a distance. Of course, when you marry into a family, you take on all those relatives as your own; yet in many ways, as an in-law, you really aren't part of the biological family. You don't share those biological ties, nor do you share the family history, particularly in the earliest years of your marriage. But just as every family has slightly different boundaries, every in-law has different wishes and needs to feel included. Please be assured that if your in-laws seem to think of you as not quite in the family, they likely aren't even aware of it.

Marissa wanted desperately to feel close to her husband's family. They spent many holidays together, she made an earnest effort to include grandparents from both sides equally, and she genuinely liked them as people. They were always very cordial, but there was a distance, a sense that Marissa wasn't really part of the family. It didn't seem to matter what Marissa did or said; it was clear that her husband was adored by his family, while she was accepted, and no more. Marissa didn't really understand what kept her in-laws from treating her as "one of them" until her husband pointed out that he had roughly the same position in her family. Everyone liked, even loved, each other, but those who had life histories and genetics in common seemed more closely connected.

This is pretty normal. Many times, young moms long to have that "family" feel with the in-laws, to be included on the same level as the biological offspring, only to be somewhat disappointed that they just don't feel as unconditionally loved. What's acceptable in a biological relative may not be so easily tolerated in an in-law. As Lily put it, "My husband could have multiple affairs, and his family would still love him; if I behaved similarly, they'd never speak to me again." Your husband and his family are bound by permanent ties; although your relationships with your in-laws can be very rich and last a lifetime, those ties are different.

When you feel left out, try to be rational. If your in-laws are actually rude to you, inviting your husband and kids to family events and intentionally leaving you out, then you and your husband should talk through how you want to handle this. Although I don't believe that this is always the best situation, many families have get-togethers in which one or another son- or daughter-in-law doesn't attend. Unless they treat you so badly that participating in family events becomes unbearable, my suggestion would be to take the high road. Be cordial and pleasant, include your in-laws in your nuclear family plans whenever feasible, attend extended family functions when invited, and hope that in time, they will see that you belong in the extended family as much as your husband does.

If your relationship with your in-laws is mostly pleasant, be grateful and leave it at that. You are lucky to care for them and enjoy them enough to want to be closer. As time goes on and you establish more family traditions together, you will become less marginal and probably also more secure. If your in-laws really seem indifferent to you (and that would be very common and even unremarkable) try not to worry about it. Remember, being treated as less than a blood relative more likely indicates their closeness to your husband, rather than any dislike of you.

My kids felt very close to my brother-in-law, but now that he and his wife are divorced, my sister wants nothing to do with him. I feel pulled in two directions. Can we maintain a close relationship with him despite the divorce?

Divorce, even when it occurs in a different household, certainly has an impact. Not only do your sister's kids have to make adjustments, you and your family do as well. This can be very hard on the extended family and friends. Just because your sister and her husband no longer want to live together doesn't mean that you no longer want to have him be involved in your life. But maintaining contact with your sister's ex can be very awkward.

You will need to work things out with your sister first. Some divorces are amicable enough to allow former in-laws to retain their close relationships. Ask your sister how she feels about you and your family keeping in touch with your former brother-in-law. If she gives you the go-ahead, then by all means, you are free to pursue that friendship. If she is uncomfortable with you staying in close touch, then you have a harder choice. Out of loyalty to your sister, you might maintain more family peace by avoiding contact.

Tamar, Abby's sister, was married for to Greg for many years. The two sisters and their husbands and children spent most holidays and birthdays together. When Tamar and Greg got divorced, Abby's kids were very upset; they felt that Greg was the one uncle with whom they had a close relationship, and they didn't want to lose his participation in their lives. In the early stages of the separation, the two families were able to remain polite, and Greg was invited to family events. As the divorce proceedings continued, though, Tamar and Greg became very bitter toward each other, and Tamar requested that Greg be left out from then on. Abby felt that she had to break ties to her former brother-in-law to maintain her relationship with her sister.

Every family handles divorce differently. If your sister can tolerate you having a separate friendship with her ex, and if all parties can remain civil about it, then go ahead and visit with Uncle Ex when your sister isn't around. If she feels too angry or demands that you sever your relationship with your kids' uncle, you may have to break contact with him to preserve the family (biological) ties.

Either way, initiate a conversation with your children about how much you all miss their uncle. Tell your kids that your sister feels uncomfortable around their former uncle, and acknowledge that while this is certainly hardest on your sister and her kids, all of you feel sad to lose a loved one to divorce. Let them talk about how they feel, express their sadness or worries, and share your feelings, too. Resist the temptation to share inappropriate stories about Uncle Ex being a total loser, thief, or womanizer, because whether or not he became a horrible person, he is still their cousins' father and their uncle, and belittling him does your children no good.

Young children especially may worry that if Aunt and Uncle stopped loving each other, Mom and Dad might, too, so you may also need to reassure your children that you are not planning to divorce (if that is true). Also, tell your kids that you are sure that Uncle Ex probably misses them as much as they miss him. If they are curious, talk to your kids about the arrangements made for their cousins to stay connected to both parents. Face your children's concerns lovingly, whatever they are, reassure them about your family's stability, and acknowledge your own feelings about missing those great extended family times, too.

Sometimes the best you can do is help your children learn to accept that sad things sometimes happen to wonderful people. No one sets out to have a marriage end in divorce, but sometimes people grow apart, and divorce is the ultimate result. Handling the issues honestly and gracefully can offer the opportunity to teach your children some important life lessons about love, marriage, and divorce. Listening to their concerns and responding appropriately can help you avoid unnecessary anxiety.

We used to spend all our holidays with my sister-in-law and her family, but now that they are separated, all our family traditions are ruined. What can I do to stop feeling so angry about this?

Unfortunately, divorce does not affect just the immediate family. Just as your kids are sad that they don't get to see the ex-relative, you are angry that your holiday celebrations must change. When a family breaks up, the repercussions reach farther than you might have thought.

Clearly, like many families in these times, your family has changed and so will your traditions. In reality, those traditions change every few years even without a divorce. A family moves to a different state, the hosting family grows too old to manage big events, the empty-nesters or elderly move to smaller, less celebration-friendly homes, young people marry and celebrate with in-laws, new babies are born, and loved ones become infirm and eventually die. Celebrations and holidays provide wonderful opportunities to reflect on these changes, both good and disappointing ones, and to consider recreating traditions to suit your new circumstances.

Accept your sadness over the loss of those special times, but remember that however sad this loss is for you, it represents a bigger change for your sister-in-law and her kids. Be supportive of her while you are all adjusting to these changes. Although she likely feels at least some relief that whatever tension or discomforts caused the separation are now in the past, she will be acutely aware that things are just not the same, and that her break-up is the reason.

Try not to dwell on the old times and help everyone move forward. You will be able to carry on some traditions just as you will have to let go of others. What's important is to get to the heart of any celebration, to focus on those of you who are still celebrating together, and appreciate what you have rather than what you've lost.

My brother got divorced, and now my kids are worried about us. I don't want them to be so scared, so how can I reassure them that we are okay?

Kids naturally worry about their own parents when other couples that seemed to be reasonably stable and content end up divorcing. If you are confident that you and your husband are not going to split up, then some reassuring is definitely in order.

- Talk about their worries. Ask what they know about divorce and give explanations that are within their understanding.
- Explain that even if parents no longer love each other, they always love their children. Occasionally, the ex-spouse does break all ties to the family, but that is never because of bad feelings about the kids; it is just that the ex can't tolerate any contact with the custodial parent.
- Make sure the children understand that children never, ever are the real cause of a divorce. Even when a child's illness or behavior challenges a couple's ability to work together and love each other well, it is the parents who cannot get along, and the parents who get divorced. The parents never divorce their kids, and the children are never to blame.
- Hearing you and your husband argue within earshot of your children may be particularly upsetting for your kids now. Teach your children that people can disagree and argue while still loving each other very much. Fighting, arguing, and disagreements are all part of living with others; they don't indicate the need or wish to separate. Reassure them that fighting doesn't mean that your marriage is in trouble. But if your fighting seems to make your

kids anxious, try to keep it from them and to a minimum for the near future.

- Help your children learn how you and your husband cope with stress and disagreements. Tell them that sometimes you walk away in a huff because you need time to sort out your feelings. Share with them how hard it is, even for grown-ups, to express disappointment or anger well, and tell them that you are trying to do it better.

- If your kids hear you arguing or screaming at each other, and if loud disagreements are simply your favorite method for getting things off your chest, explain that you and Daddy occasionally disagree about things, and that arguing often helps you to find ways to compromise. Make sure they know that you and Dad often resolve things by these loud arguments, and that it sounds much worse than it is. Reassure them that this is just your style, and nothing to worry them.

- Tell your offspring that sometimes your feelings get confused or hurt, there are misunderstandings even between people who love each other very much, and you and Dad are working to understand each other better and be kinder to each other.

- Ask your children to describe their concerns about your marriage and respond to each child according to his or her questions and ability to understand your answers.

- Remember that some children want lengthy explanations and others want simple facts with no embellishments. Don't answer any more than what they ask. Gear your answers to their ability to understand.

- Talk about your strong commitment to your husband, his to you, and your mutual commitment to making your family life as good as possible. If your marriage is solid, tell your kids, show them by behaving in loving and respectful ways toward each other.

Particularly while the children are adjusting to the idea of their beloved uncle getting divorced, be visibly kind and loving in your own marriage, and relate to each other in ways that support each other. Although it's important to allow your children to ask questions and to talk about their feelings about a family divorce, you must also reassure your children by your behavior that you are going to stay together. Talk to your kids about their worries and try to demonstrate that yours is a contented marriage. Showing your children that you love each other and that you plan to work on any issues that come up between you will be the best reassurance of all.

I love my sister, but she is raising her kids so differently than we are. I feel guilty every time I turn down an invitation from her or don't include her family in our activities, but our kids just don't get along together; they have very different attitudes and values. Should we keep seeing them?

If you love your sister and still do well together, but the children don't get along, the easiest approach to this problem is to continue seeing your sister individually and cut back on the whole-family visits. That way you maintain your close and loving relationship with your sister, but you decrease opportunities for stress and tension among the kids. Pamela had a similar problem. She and her husband raised their boys and girls very similarly, encouraging each to reach the highest levels of education possible, offering lots of classes and travel experiences, and generally expecting great things from them. Pamela's sister, however, split household chores clearly along gender lines, with daughters learning to baby-sit and cook, and sons doing heavy labor and pursuing academic interests. The parents got along despite these ideological differences, but the kids had a lot of trouble even finding something to talk about. They cut their time together as a family to annual family visits and took the attitude that their children learned a lot from seeing how differently their cousins were being raised.

I would hesitate to eliminate *all* visits among the children. Part of life involves learning to get along with lots of different types of people and understanding that there are different religions, goals, and lifestyles, all of which are equally valuable. Maintaining limited contact by celebrating a couple of holidays each year together allows the children to see how each family lives and get a taste of the others' choices, both as opportunities and limitations. These visits could provide for rich conversations as your children become aware of other ways to live. Although there will certainly continue to be awkward times, showing your children that you can love someone with vastly dissimilar attitudes and values provides a valuable opportunity.

Continue to see your sister, but don't require your children to spend every weekend with these cousins. Limit the whole-family visits to a few times a year if they are truly too awkward, but encourage your children to become tolerant and accepting of other points of view.

As long as your sister or her kids are not trying to convince you that their lifestyle is decidedly better, don't dwell on your opposing viewpoints. Families can be very unlike each other, yet still offer great love and life lessons. Enjoy your differences and use them to help your children think about the world a bit more deeply.

We have an unmarried relative whom I love, but she is cohabitating with a lover rather than getting married. I feel guilty keeping my kids away from her, but how can we visit with her without the children thinking we condone this behavior?

In the twenty-first century, whether you like it or not, your children will be exposed to many different life choices. Television, newspaper, magazines, and movies all show a variety of relationships. Many more adults are cohabiting rather than marrying, including many older couples, and, in general, there is much greater societal acceptance of these non-married decisions. If you do not condone cohabitation, you have every right to teach your children your values, but you can do so in such a way as to maintain a relationship with your relative who clearly has different ideas.

These days, many couples cohabit, and they are not all young people. When older couples with grown children from earlier marriages fall in love, they are increasingly choosing to live together without getting married, as the legal marriage complicates how each will be able to will their estates to their own children. If your children are very little, they won't notice or care whether or not Grandma and Elliot are married. What matters to them is that Grandma and Elliot are fun to be around, and that they are happy.

As the kids get older, they may question the relationship, but they also may not. It is up to you to teach them the value of love and marriage and to pass along your values. If a cohabiting couple comes for an overnight visit, you get to decide how to handle the sleeping arrangements. The age of your children and the relative permanence or seriousness of the relationship may dictate whether or not you allow an unmarried couple to sleep in the same room in your home.

My suggestion is to avoid making too big a deal out of this. Cohabitation is increasingly common and tolerated, and creating a family rift, or being judgmental about someone else's life choices, teaches your children more about your lack of tolerance than about what you consider positive values. You must come to terms with other people making different life choices than you and help your children do the same.

If this relationship really makes you uncomfortable—and you feel that exposing your children to this couple teaches your kids that you approve of their living arrangement—then only visit with these relatives on neutral territory. Talk with your children about why you feel that making a legal commitment is important. Explain why some people make different choices. But most importantly, live your life honestly. If you talk to your children about why you make the choices you do and are tolerant of others' choices, you will raise good kids who feel able to make decisions that are best for them. Being too rigid and restrictive, or condemning others doesn't really work.

My mother was widowed a few years ago and now she's dating. I resent having to include her dates in our family events. What should I do?

There are really two issues affecting other family members when a beloved relative starts dating, whether after a divorce or following a death. First, the whole extended family must get used to the idea that this relative is ready to move on and prepare themselves to welcome a new mate to the family. Second, each family must sort out when a new partner is permanent enough to be included in family events.

As much as we all want our loved ones to be happy, it can be really awkward and uncomfortable to see your own mother flirting, dating, and showering affection on some man who is not your father. Even when your dad has been gone for a respectable amount of time, and even when, objectively, you want your mother to find love again, watching her actively becoming emotionally involved with another man can make you feel quite ill at ease. You may feel that Mom is being disloyal, or if you like the new gentleman caller, you may feel disloyal. If your discomfort with Mom's dating is connected to your not yet being ready to let go of your dad (or in the case of divorce, the wish that Mom and Dad will eventually reunite), you need to do some serious soul-searching. Your mom is single, and if she is ready to start a new phase and new relationships, she will need your support.

Developing a true affection for your mother's new man takes a lot of time, though. Just because your mother likes or even loves this new guy doesn't mean that you will. Take your time, be cordial and friendly, and allow yourself to get to know this new man. If your mother likes him, there has to be something good there, right? And keep in mind that if your mother is happy, you should at least be pleased for her. Look for the good qualities and be grateful that your mother has the potential for happiness.

In terms of when to include the new man in your family celebrations, I honestly believe that this should be mostly up to your mother to decide. When she feels ready to bring him along, he should be invited. At any event that you would include "and guest" on an invitation, Mom should be allowed to bring along her version of that guest. If there is a more intimate, family-only activity, you may want to discuss with Mom whether or not she wants to include her new friend. Be open-minded and inclusive whenever possible. If Mom wants her new friend, be welcoming and friendly.

Ideally, Grandma will find a mate she loves, and you will all love him, too. Many lives, not just your mother's, can be enriched by this new relationship. Face your own feelings about the loss of your dad, talk with your kids about theirs, and relax. Your mom deserves your support while she develops her new life. You can all maintain the love and respect you had for your father while still welcoming your mother's new friend or love. You will all feel better if you do.

My children's grandmother wants to baby-sit, but I don't think she is capable. How can I keep her from baby-sitting without hurting her feelings?

Nicole's mother-in-law had been a lively, warm, and enthusiastic baby-sitter in her early grandparenting days, but as she got older, she developed numerous medical problems that left her somewhat hard of hearing and much less agile. As much as Nicole loved her, she worried that this grandma was not up to taking care of a lively four-year-old. Nicole solved this by telling her mother-in-law that she had earned the right to have just the fun parts of grandparenthood. She also flattered the grandmother by telling her that she wants time to see her, too. Whenever this grandmother offered to baby-sit, Nicole thanked her politely and instead scheduled a visit. Nicole would be around to supervise, and Grandma got to spend time with her grandchild.

Jessica had a similarly limited mother who also wanted to help her out by baby-sitting. Jessica's solution was to hire a baby-sitter or housekeeper to be in the home when Grandma was supposedly baby-sitting. That way, Jessica got some time off, Grandma got to have a mostly private visit with her granddaughter, and there was another adult in the house who could be called upon in an emergency or to help Grandma with the more physically demanding aspects of child care.

Both of these suggestions help the aging grandparent maintain her dignity and self-respect while also encouraging positive interaction with the grandkids. As people live longer, there are lots more opportunities for children to get to know their grandparents, and having grandma and grandpa baby-sit, when it works, is a great way to give you a break *and* secure their relationship. But if Grandma truly isn't up to it in your estimation, you must do what you feel protects your child. Do not have Grandma baby-sit if you feel she can't handle it. But also be careful, loving, and creative in helping this grandmother visit with your kids.

Your children benefit when you manage this situation well. You show them compassion when you treat the elderly or infirm with respect. You show that you value your relative by arranging many visits. And you will feel that your children are safe while they are developing a loving relationship with this grandparent. You all win.

My kids have three sets of grandparents: my mother and her husband, my father and his wife, and my in-laws, and they all seem to be competitive about who is the best grandparent. How can I get them to behave themselves?

Sometimes, even supposedly mature people act like little kids. I've heard many stories about how sets of grandparents compete for favored grandparent status. It's laughable, except when it's your kids who are being pushed and pulled to visit more often, or who are showered with unnecessary and lavish gifts in the attempt at winning their affection. When there are ex-spouses and multiple sets of interested relatives, the competition can get dicey.

Talk to them, if at all possible. Tell them that you want your children to love all their relatives and have great relationships with them all. Remind them that grandparenting is not a competitive sport. Reassure the grandparents that you totally support their desire to feel connected to your children. Ask them to limit gifts because you don't want your kids to learn to expect gifts from grandparents; you *do* want them to love them, enjoy them, and maybe expect to learn something or to have fun together.

Do not talk about one set of grandparents to the others. If your father-in-law asks you who bought Brooke that beautiful dress (and it was your father), jump up out of your seat, exclaiming "I almost forgot; I have to make a call!" and leave the room. Or ignore the question, responding instead, "Don't you think Brooke's eyes look just like yours?" If they want to know how often you visit with the other grandparents, tell them you try to see all of the relatives as much as possible. Learn to change the subject if they try to compare gifts or involvement. Remind them that your children love and enjoy them. Teach them that loving relationships can't be compared or measured, and tell them you are grateful that so many people love your children.

If you allow frequent visits, phone calls, and email; eliminate their ability to measure each other's generosity or contact; and deflect the competitive questions, you will go a long way in decreasing the competition among these relatives. You will also teach your children that love is not something you can measure, that the richness of a relationship comes from the closeness the people feel rather than the gifts that they give, and that you value people for who they are, not for what they do. These are very good lessons.

Chapter Five

Motherhood and Friendship

Mandy and Lani had been best friends since high school, despite being very different people. Fifteen years out of high school, Mandy was unmarried, a high level executive, and totally career-oriented, while Lani, married with two children, loved taking care of her home and family, and was very involved in her community. Before Lani had kids, they would spend a lot of quality time together. Lani thoroughly enjoyed following Mandy's travels and career, and Mandy felt at peace visiting Lani's home. Their friendship thrived during the early years of Lani's marriage despite living in different states; there were visits to each other's towns, long phone calls, and lots of emails. Mandy was frequently a guest in Lani's home, and Lani, her husband, and Mandy would go out together whenever Mandy was in town.

Trouble began, though, when Lani began having children. She was no longer able to talk at length, without interruptions, on the telephone, or to stay out late midweek when Mandy flew in to see her. Sometimes Mandy wanted Lani to get a baby-sitter and spend a Saturday with her when Lani really wanted to be with her family. Lani felt that Mandy didn't understand that her two young children took a great deal of her time, and that baby-sitters weren't always available. Mandy felt that Lani was no longer very interested in her, that she was too focused on her kids and not much fun anymore. Sadly, there were a lot of hurt feelings on both sides, as neither felt that the other had adjusted very graciously to the changes in Lani's life. Mandy felt that Lani no longer cared about her and Lani felt that Mandy was unreasonably demanding.

Veronica and Andrea met in their childbirth class and delivered their first daughters within weeks of each other. They became fast friends, spending several days a week together over the course of the babies' first years. As the girls got older and the moms got to know each other better, they discovered that they had a lot less in common than they had originally thought. Once the children became mobile and started to interact a bit more actively, it became clear that the two women had wildly different ideas about child rearing, politics, you name it. While they were both consumed with keeping their babies alive and getting accustomed to getting too little sleep and never making it anywhere on time, their friendship flourished. When the intensity and desperate need for companionship of early motherhood faded, so did their friendship.

Edie and Sylvie were best friends in preschool, so their mothers spent a lot of time together, too, arranging play dates, going on field trips together, and carpooling. The girls went on to different elementary schools, got involved with their new school chums, and their friendship naturally loosened and ultimately dissolved, but their mothers had become quite close. Edie and Sylvie are in college now and have no contact with each other, but their mothers see each other all the time.

Some friendships survive major life changes, and others struggle or fade away. Some friendships are meant to last a lifetime, some ebb and flow as one or the other's life circumstances bring the friends closer or further apart, and other close relationships dissolve when it becomes clear that the pals no longer have much in common. And many mothers develop wonderful friendships through their children. It's one of the side benefits to parenthood; you get to meet a wide variety of people you might otherwise never have known, share in the rearing of each other's children, and often develop warm and satisfying ties.

Motherhood causes some enormous shifts in how a woman lives her life, including how she sets priorities, what time she has available for socializing, her financial comfort, her interests, and her energy level. Motherhood often clarifies a woman's values, makes her think about what she needs as well as what she wants to give the world; these shifts may change what a woman wants from her friends as well as what she is able to offer a friendship.

Women need friends, and women who are mothers need friends even more. But women often experience their motherhood differently than each other, and some non-mothers have trouble maintaining their friendships with their friends who are mothers because their lives are so different. Some women are open to a wider variety of people, while some want to close ranks and surround themselves only with like-minded folks going through the same things at the same times. Some women, when they become mothers, find that they need to rethink their old friendships, some find formerly casual acquaintances to be more appealing, fun, understanding, or generous than they'd ever imagined, and a few find that formerly close friends seem to have lost all interest in them.

Motherhood demands a lot of a woman, as does friendship. Finding the time and energy to devote to friends is important, but even important friendships can all too easily be overlooked or neglected when you are run ragged just taking care of your family. Many moms realize that although they used to be very nurturing to their friends, they are completely "nurtured out" at home, and what they need from or are capable of giving to their friends now may be very different than it used to be. Still, even when a friendship is no longer satisfying to either party, it's very painful when it falters.

When a mother is deeply involved in her own life, she needs her friends, but also may find it difficult to keep up with them. She may feel guilty when she repeatedly forgets to return a call, or if her children's or family's needs seem always to preempt her time with her buddies. She may also feel rebuffed or wonder what she did wrong if a friend stops calling her. Sometimes when a woman's friends aren't mothers themselves, the friendship flounders; their needs, interests, and availability may be too dissimilar to sustain the closeness.

This chapter considers many ways in which friendships enrich a mom's life, but also discusses the difficulties moms sometimes have figuring out when to pursue a friendship and when to let one go. It looks at what mothers do or don't do to maintain and nourish their friendships, at how different values or parenting styles may impact your relationships, and offers suggestions to help you get through some of the most frequent friendship issues, like jealousy and competitiveness.

Just as people grow and change over time, so do friendships; I think this may be the most important thing I've learned from working with mothers and considering how motherhood and friendship coexist. A friendship might be tremendously gratifying and meaningful at one point in your life, but not be able to continue to meet your needs as your lives diverge. I also came to understand that usually no one is at fault; as life experiences and circumstances change, needs change, and sometimes the ability or desire to fill those needs disappears. Sometimes your interests become just too dissimilar to make the friendship workable. Some people are more tolerant and accepting of disagreements and differences than others.

While it's true that mothers really need their friends, it is also true that motherhood changes a woman, and those changes may impact a friendship. This chapter looks at the ways motherhood and friendship affect each other. It should help you make the most of your most important relationships and come to terms with friendships that may disappoint.

I focus so much energy on my work and family, I've allowed my relationships to slide. How can I avoid feeling totally friendless and still be an attentive wife and mother?

It's easy to get so caught up in the day-to-day demands of work and family that you forget to schedule in time with friends, but having friends and maintaining outside interests can actually help you be a more fulfilled, and therefore, better, wife, worker, and mother. Lots of things may be contributing to your withdrawal from the social scene, from worry that you'll bore your friends to feeling genuinely and completely fulfilled by taking care of your job and family. But if you are concerned that you're becoming a recluse, then you need to find ways to stay close to the people you still care about and make new friends who will be compatible with you and understanding of your current lifestyle.

Fortunately you live in an era in which keeping in touch is easier than ever:

-❧ Use the Internet to check in with friends. You can email or respond to a friend any time of day or night, whenever you have a few minutes. You can even start a note and finish it later if family or duty calls.

- Get a hands-free telephone, or an earpiece for your current phone, so that you can talk with friends while you commute to or from work, or while folding laundry.
- Invite a friend for spontaneous, last minute get-togethers. You don't need a reason, entertainment, or a lavish spread to see your pals.
- Be creative about when, and under what circumstance, you visit with friends. Invite a friend to keep you company while you run errands, take a yoga class together, or go out for an early breakfast.
- If you genuinely can't find the time to see your friends, at least tell them that you care and that you hope that they will understand that you'll want to be with them as soon as you are able. Do your best to maintain telephone or email contact at least a few times a year.
- If you feel that you no longer have much in common with your old friends, make new ones. Join a class or speak to the friendly moms in the park or at the coffee house. Invite a neighbor over for tea.
- Develop friendships with coworkers. Go out to lunch together and talk about things other than work. Start a book group or a cooking club at work so that your professional friends become social friends.
- There are plenty of Internet sites through which you can meet like-minded people. It may not be the same as meeting someone face-to-face, but many Internet friendships can be very satisfying and may take less time away from your other pursuits.

Even if you currently feel no need to socialize now, if you raise your kids to become confident and independent people, before too long, you will have a lot more free time; you are likely to want to use at least some of that time to see your friends. Invest some time in your social life *now*; make sure that the people you care about stay in your life, and if you want new friends, take the risk and meet new people. Your work and family may always come first, but friends offer a different and equally important satisfaction. It will be worth the effort, both immediately and in the long run, to keep your social life alive.

I feel guilty that I don't keep up with old friends, but how can I make that work when my life is so different than theirs?

Many women who marry and/or have children years before or after the majority of their friends do find it hard to maintain those friendships. Particularly if the way you socialized before children included late nights out, going to bars, theatre, weekend trips, or lengthy and uninterrupted visits, staying close to friends who have a great deal more free time and flexibility than you have can be difficult. When a woman becomes thoroughly ensconced in her own family and work life, her needs, interests, and availability to hang out can change. And when those needs change, sometimes she is surprised and may be disappointed to discover that it's impossible to sustain a friendship that she'd thought would last forever.

At this time in your life, you not only need friends—you want friends who will understand that your priorities, availability, and interests have changed, and you crave friends who are comfortable accommodating to your current emotional and practical situation.

It also helps to have friends who are able to relate to your immediate circumstances and concerns. Figuring out which friendships are worth the extra effort and how to make new friends who share your interests can be daunting, but if you can develop a rewarding social life, you'll never be sorry.

If certain friendships seem to have suffered since your life has become so full, find ways to reconnect.

- Invite friends over for informal events, pot luck meals, or even to take your kids to the zoo or a museum, regardless of whether your friends have kids or not. If your kids are entertained, you may be better able to attend to your friend.
- Hire a sitter or leave the kids with your husband while you go out with your chum one-on-one, thereby guaranteeing uninterrupted time with the friend. More than one friendship has been lost because the mom was unable or unwilling to hire a sitter.
- Use the Internet to maintain contact. That way you can write long notes when you have the time, and your friends won't be annoyed by frequent interruptions.
- Accept that some friendships may not survive your different life choices and availability.

As your family becomes more independent, so will you. Your social life will once again center on sharing emotional bonds rather than being on the same nap schedule or shift at work. Until then, nurture whatever relationships seem worthy, develop new ones, and go easy on yourself. Your social life is meant to be enjoyable and supportive, not give you something else to feel bad about.

Some of my friends seem to have everything and do it all well and effortlessly. I am embarrassed to admit it, but I am jealous. How can I handle this green-eyed monster without ruining my relationships?

When admiration or affection turns to jealousy, there are problems. Some friendships survive and become even closer when both friends can recognize and work through the discomforts, but for others, the jealousy indicates a "disconnect" between the two buddies that may not be bridged. You need to sort out whether your envy reflects your own insecurities or whether you and your friend have expectations, emotions, and experiences that are just too much at odds with each other. When you understand what is causing the friction between you, you can decide how to proceed.

Lucy's friend, Vicky, was the epitome of perfection, and sadly, the object of Lucy's envy. Two weeks after delivering her second baby, Vicky invited Lucy over for lunch. To Lucy's amazement, Vicky's house was immaculate, her newborn on a schedule, and her makeup tastefully applied. Lucy, pregnant with her second child, stared in shock as Vicki prepared a lovely meal and calmly enjoyed the conversation. Lucy admired Vicky's ability to handle everything so graciously, but felt more than a bit jealous, as she was convinced that she herself would not be able to function that well in the same situation.

In talking about this friendship, Lucy moaned that she would never measure up to Vicky's calm and organized approach to motherhood and life. But Lucy didn't feel comfortable talking to Vicky about her feelings. She felt that Vicky would judge her; that Vicky wouldn't be able to relate to her messier, more emotional, way of handling her life, and that she couldn't relate to Vicky's ability or need to be totally in control. The more I heard about

Vicky's accomplishments, and Lucy's supposed lack thereof, the more I became convinced that this friendship was not meant to be. These two women had opposing approaches to handling stress and even more different ideas about what kinds of emotions you share in a friendship. Lucy wanted to talk about what she found difficult while Vicky needed to show how well she was managing.

To get past the green-eyed monster, you need to examine what's causing this unwelcome emotion. Jealousy is often more about how you're feeling about yourself than about how perfect your sister or neighbor is. Are you disappointed in yourself? Did you expect to be more efficient, more in love with your children, more adept at juggling your various responsibilities than you are? If you are not meeting your own expectations, and it appears that your best friend is exceeding them, your jealousy may actually be more a reflection of your self-doubt than a true resentment of your good friend. And if you are the object of a friend's envy, you might want to consider why you need to appear so accomplished, or what blocks you from sharing your insecurities or innermost thoughts with your friends.

True friends share both the highs and lows of life. Closeness develops from the honest but kindly exchange of ideas, emotions, and experiences. Good friends care much more about who you are as a person than how well you do things. You shouldn't feel that you must be superhuman to maintain your friendships, because true friends don't judge you.

Don't assume that your friend who seems to have it all together isn't feeling just as stressed as you are, or that you should be anything other than you are. If you can, talk about how you feel with your friend. Clear the air and try to face your own feelings about motherhood. Come to terms with who you are and how good a mother you are—and avoid the comparisons. You are probably each trying to be the best moms you can be, and there are lots of ways for each of you to be great. Besides, jealousy does no one any good. So let it go.

My friends want to see me without my children. Why don't they understand that sometimes I can't or don't want to spend money for a sitter?

As much as you want to maintain your old friendships, your interests and priorities are different now that you're a mom. It's hard to maintain some friendships when your lifestyle or life stage is dramatically different. If you are the only one in your circle of friends who either has young children or doesn't use a sitter very often, the way you want to socialize may no longer be compatible with theirs.

Sally and Noelle had been close friends for years. When Noelle moved to a new home, she invited Sally and her husband, Steve, over for Sunday brunch, asking them to leave the kids at home. Sally, unable to find a sitter after several attempts, asked if she could instead bring them along. Although Noelle said yes, it was clear she was annoyed, and later told Sally that she was really upset that they never could be together as adults. Neither Sally nor Noelle was wrong; they just wanted different things. Sally thought she had tried hard enough to get a sitter, and that getting together with her kids in tow would be better than canceling the date, while Noelle wanted a more elegant, adults-only visit. Sally was hurt that Noelle considered her children a burden, while Noelle felt Sally was being inconsiderate. These two friends were just in very different places in their lives, neither understanding the others' needs or priorities.

You want and expect good friends to support and understand you, even when your choices may not be the same as theirs. You don't want them to be judgmental of you for doing things your own way, or to push you to do anything that doesn't seem right to you. It's painful to discover that people you felt close to don't embrace your new life and choices as warmly as you'd hoped. If best friends balk when you bring your baby along, or are disappointed that you'd rather have them accompany you to the park so your kids can play while you chat, then the friendship may suffer, and in some cases end. This doesn't indicate that you or your friends are terrible people; it just means that your friendship may not have been as solid as you'd thought.

Some friendships weather these storms, regaining their closeness when the friends have similar lifestyles, either because the non-mother eventually has children of her own or because the kids grow up. Other friendships dissolve as the friends discover that the differences in how they spend their time or make choices about child care or work indicate that their values are too dissimilar for comfort. Making different choices doesn't always doom a relationship, but when those differences reflect dramatically different values or are experienced by one friend as critical of the other, the friendship probably wasn't as close or healthy as you'd believed it to be.

Be patient. Let friendships wax and wane, as they naturally will. If someone really hurts you, you can certainly open up a dialog about the issue, but often time will solve rifts in a friendship if they are minor and ease the pain if the relationship disintegrates. Although it may hurt, no one is to blame when two people have different needs and ideas about friendship.

My close friend's child teases and taunts my child; my child is scared of hers, and I can't stand it. I feel terrible, but how can I protect both my child and my friendship?

This question reminds me of two of the hardest lessons I had to learn as a mother of young children. First, it became clear that no matter how much I wanted it, my children and my friends' children might not become close friends. Second, sometimes people who were my friends might have very different ideas about how to parent their kids, and those ideas reflected values that I didn't much like. I had always assumed that people I like would treat their children the way I would, handle misbehaviors similarly, and we'd all just get along great. Mostly, it's been true, but occasionally, friendships between adults don't lead to friendships between children, and seeing your friend as a parent can disappoint.

No matter how close you and your friend are, though, your first responsibility is to your child. Ideally, you and your friend will both recognize that what goes on between your children isn't good for either of them. Talk to your friend about your concerns. Present your impressions of how you think the kids behave together in a kind and constructive tone. Approach the problem as one that needs solving for both kids, emphasizing that your child needs to be better able to defend himself, and her child needs to be more aware that what he is doing hurts other kids. Together you and your friend can continue to monitor how the kids treat each other, and both your kids' friendship and yours will be strengthened. In addition, your child will see that he or she shouldn't tolerate being treated badly, and the other child will learn that teasing hurts.

Of course, the ideal isn't always possible. Many moms don't want to face the less appealing sides of their own children. Some are offended at the mere mention that Frankie isn't absolutely perfect. Some will see the same situation very differently than you, perhaps saying that your child asks for such treatment, that the teasing isn't so bad, or that she believes that the children should learn to manage these little squabbles themselves—without adult interference. If telling your friend that you feel that your kids have trouble getting along leads to an indignant response, if she blames your child or minimizes your child's discomfort, or if you are fearful that mentioning this issue will destroy your friendship, you have a bigger problem. Then you will need to help your child more actively manage or avoid the teasing on his own, you may decide to limit the contact between the children, and you may also want to reconsider this friendship.

If your friend's response seems too much out of keeping with your own ideas and values, then you may have to figure out how you feel about this relationship. What does this friendship really mean to you? Does your history together make finding peace between you worth your discomfort with your friend's parenting style? Can you keep this friendship on a more fun level, rather than a heart-to-heart, soul-sister, and best friend level? Are you comfortable being friends with people whose values are very different than yours? Does the way your friend deals with your concerns about your kids reflect a gap between you that you don't want to bridge? If your friendship can't sustain this glitch, then it probably wasn't as deep as you would have liked. It may be time to let the relationship go through a natural cooling down period, and maybe let it go altogether.

What's important is that you assess the situation as objectively as possible, which can be very hard when both friendship and parenthood are in the mix. Try to be honest with yourself, your kids, and your friend about how you feel, about what happens between the kids, and try to work together to solve the problem. Remember that your primary responsibility is to protect and guide your child. Truly good friends and real soul mates will want to work this out with you. With a lot of honesty and tact, you might be able to save both your child and your friendship.

One of my good friends so obviously favors one of her children that it makes me very uncomfortable. Is it awful that I don't want to be friends with someone who treats her kids so unfairly?

It's not at all awful, but it can sometimes be very sad and uncomfortable to witness when a parent favors one child over another. It's also sad to recognize that how your friend treats her kids might imply some things about your friend you'd rather not have known about her. While nobody treats each of her children exactly the same, when you see your friend clearly favoring one child over another, it's painful to watch, and hard to know what, if anything, to do.

Some friendships are close and trusting enough to tolerate it when one friend confronts the other with constructive criticism. If you are right about your friend's partiality to the one child, it would certainly be in your friend's children's best interest to help her recognize and eliminate the unfair and unequal treatment. Gently pointing out that she seems to be more lenient or affectionate with the one child might help her see how her behavior may be affecting all of her children, and she might be grateful and change her ways. Then the problem would be solved.

The difficulty is in being sure that what you are seeing does in fact exist, and that talking to your friend about it would be helpful. If you don't have a great deal of contact with your friend and her kids, what you see as favoritism might be a one- or two-time incident, a result of something specific going on in the family about which you know nothing, and therefore not at all indicative of a bigger problem. Perhaps the seemingly favored child had just experienced a major disappointment, and what you saw as favoritism was the Mom's way of boosting that child's self-esteem that particular day.

However, if you have evidence that this child routinely gains more privileges, affection, and always seems favored, then you must decide if confronting your friend will do any good. Many moms do not respond well when their friends criticize their mothering. No matter how well-intended you are, talking about what you believe is your friend's poor parenting could damage your friendship forever. You must weigh your willingness to jeopardize the friendship with your discomfort about seeing the kids treated unfairly.

My experience has been that it takes very strong women and very trusting friends to be able to give or take constructive criticism at all well, especially about something as personal and emotionally loaded as parenting. If you are absolutely certain that this friend is hurting her children by her biased parenting, if you are willing to sacrifice the friendship, if necessary, to protect the children, or if you realize that you'd rather lose the friendship than keep quiet, talk to your friend about your concerns. Find a time when you and your friend are alone, describe the behaviors that worry you, and be willing to listen to her reaction. Be supportive but clear, and be prepared for your friend to be upset, possibly very angry, with you.

Many women will choose to either end or cool off this friendship rather than confront a friend who may be parenting her children badly. Honestly, I'm not sure that retreating is such a bad response. Although in principle, I believe it is best to be direct with your feelings and share your concerns openly, I also know that many friendships cannot tolerate that much unedited, critical honesty. You must follow your heart, both about how much this friendship means to you and about how worried you are about the children.

Friendship and parenthood are both difficult but rewarding experiences. You must do what you feel is right, for yourself as well as for others. If you speak up and your friend is angry, the worst you've done is found out that your friend may not be the person you had hoped she was. The best might be that you and she will become closer, and she will become a better mother as a result of your comments.

One of my good friends has very different ideas about how to discipline children. Is it bad that I don't want to hang out with her and her kids anymore?

Miranda and Samantha met in a baby exercise class when their sons were newborns, and the two moms and the two babies spent a lot of time together in those first several months of motherhood. Miranda and Sam became pregnant with their second babies at just about the same time, and this is when some problems began. Miranda told her first child about the pregnancy immediately, while Samantha wanted to delay telling her son until a bit further along. The boys were by now talkative toddlers, and as such had their own ideas about many things, including whether or not they wanted to take turns, to share, or to listen to the other, and the moms had even more different ideas about how to discipline them. Miranda was very stern, setting strict limits and spanking her son if he broke family rules, while

Samantha believed in explaining why rules are important and talking through squabbles until everyone understood. As their children grew up, their very different parenting styles became clearer, and, it seemed to the two moms, those styles reflected extremely different views and values. The mothers' friendship slowly dissolved.

Many friendships develop among women whose kids are friends; sometimes these friendships are based more on the children's compatibility than on the moms', and that's perfectly fine. The problems arise when the moms assume that they have more in common than they do, and become disappointed when they discover that while their children might be good friends, the moms really aren't suited a close relationship. When the mothers have spent enough time together to have a clearer idea about what each other values, they realize that they have less in common than they'd hoped. The mothers' friendship may then fizzle.

This doesn't mean that you must agree with everything another mom says or does in order to be good friends. Many close relationships thrive on the differences between them. But when watching your friend respond to her child makes you uncomfortable, or when the other mother's discipline techniques reflect a value system that is too unlike yours, a close bond is hard to maintain. One of the trickiest things about parenting is that some things work for some people and not for others. Just because you don't agree or handle problems similarly doesn't mean that either you or your friend is a bad parent—but you may not be compatible.

If your discipline approaches are so different that you can't tolerate being with this family, gradually withdraw from the adult relationship while still supporting your children's friendship. As the children get older, it will become natural to make dates for just the kids; offer to be the supervising parent, be cordial to the other mother, and the friendship between the children can thrive while you and the other mom grow more distant.

Remember, you don't have to be friends with everyone. Helping your child maintain his relationship with a cherished friend while you choose the friends you most enjoy helps you feel more at ease and teaches your child that you support his friendships, too.

My best friend says that I "stole" her favorite baby-sitter. How can I deal with how angry she is and how guilty I feel about it?

You would have been better off stealing her husband! Of course you feel guilty and of course she is angry. Your friend did you a favor by letting you "borrow" her favorite baby-sitter, and you stole her away. Even if the baby-sitter prefers to sit for your kids, you have breached an often unspoken rule of motherhood: Never, ever, ever steal a baby-sitter! You have learned the hard way how precious a commodity a cherished baby-sitter is. You have some friendship repair work to do.

If you still value this friendship, and if your friend is still willing to talk to you, be honest and forthright about what happened. Admit that you were so impressed with Claire's baby-sitting skills that, without thinking first, you asked her to be your regular Saturday-night sitter. Even if your friend and the sitter didn't have an agreement that she was "their" sitter, acknowledge that you should have asked your friend first. Offer to undo the damage by releasing Claire from her commitment to you. Grovel, apologize, and never do this to anyone else again, and hope that your friend understands and forgives you.

Beg your friend's forgiveness and ask her to ask the fabulous sitter if she has any similarly reliable and charming friends who could baby-sit for you. In the future, if you use a sitter who routinely sits for someone else, be clear about loyalties and expectations. Never steal a friend's sitter, and when you find your own phenomenal sitter, be generous, but also very specific about your expectations if you ever share her number with a friend.

One of my childless friends gets annoyed with me whenever I have to hang up the phone abruptly if my baby cries or my toddler needs me. Should I feel guilty that I often take care of my kids rather than staying on the phone?

Your friend calls you when she's on her coffee break; she doesn't realize that when you're home with kids, you're at your work but you don't *get* coffee breaks. Despite the fact that it seems obvious to you, a mom, that when your baby cries or your toddler bumps her head, you need to go to him or her immediately, to your non-mom friend, ending a phone call abruptly evidently seems rude. She may feel that you are choosing your kids over her, or that you are overindulgent by responding to them rather than continuing your conversation. Your friend's reaction may make you wonder if you should make your kids learn to respect your telephone time, or it may lead you to question your friend's maturity, as she seems to compete with your kids for your attention. You don't need to feel guilty, though, unless you are hanging up on your friend constantly, whether your kids really need you or not.

Lara and Stacy had been friends since high school. When Lara had children, though, things seemed to change. Stacy wanted to spend time alone with Lara. Because Lara worked full time, when she socialized, she preferred to bring her kids along. Stacy felt that Lara had become too child-focused and didn't seem interested in her anymore, while Lara felt that Stacy was being demanding and immature, expecting her to put her kids' needs second to Stacy's. The friendship dissolved over time, largely because these two women no longer could meet each other's needs and expectations. Their priorities and values had grown too far apart.

Childless people are often clueless as to what it takes to keep young children alive and content. As a mother, your childless friends may also sometimes seem as childish as your kids, demanding your attention whenever your children do. To be completely fair, though, mothers sometimes become so devoted to their kids that they stop nurturing certain friendships adequately. As a good friend *and* mother, you understandably feel torn between wanting to take care of your children and wanting to be there for your friends. Sometimes it's hard to do both.

Talk to your friend. Help her understand that sometimes you simply must help your kids immediately; bloody knees and drippy diapers just can't wait. Call your friend back as soon as possible after dealing with the interruption and explain what happened. Apologize for the interruption (not for taking care of your kids) and resume the conversation. If you value the friendship, make time to see your friend or chat on the phone or online when someone else is in charge of the kids.

If these efforts don't satisfy your friend, it may mean that the friendship will not survive the different life choices you each have made. If you need to be less close for awhile, or if your shifting priorities and behaviors are so painful for either of you that feelings are too hurt, you might have to come to terms with the fact that this friendship is not what you'd thought it was. While that may be disappointing and sad, not all friendships are meant to last forever. Sometimes it seems easier to feel guilty that your behavior angers your friend than it is to face losing the friendship. But to my mind, if apologizing for interruptions doesn't satisfy your friend, then your friend doesn't really understand you and your life, and the friendship isn't as mutual and lasting as you'd hoped. So stop feeling guilty and do what you can to repair the friendship, but keep in mind that not all friendships may be able to be repaired.

I have a friend who constantly "complains" about how hard it is to raise such a talented and gifted child as hers. Is it bad that I don't want to listen to her gripe about the difficulties of driving from one advanced class to another?

When friends "complain" about how hard it is that little Francesca is walking and talking nonstop at only nine months old, or moan and groan about the struggle their son is having trying to choose between becoming a concert violinist or an Olympic level gymnast, your patience can be tried. These are not problems; they are opportunities. Unfortunately, in some circles, bragging about your kids is forbidden, while complaining is not. So the bragging, sometimes unconsciously, takes the form of a burden, something to be endured rather than enjoyed or simply experienced.

A woman I know used to talk like this all the time. In reality, her kids were pretty great, but her life as an individual was also relatively dull. Rather than complain that she was bored, or unsatisfied, she seemed to make a career out of her children's lives, to find drama in daily activities. Once, when her son had a formal event to attend, she described the day as a disaster because just as they were getting ready to leave, she discovered he'd outgrown his only pair of dress pants. Everything was always a big deal to her, even though she was financially stable, her marriage solid, and her kids all healthy and smart. Sometimes people who seem to be complaining about their children's accomplishments aren't trying to brag; they just don't have enough going on in their own lives, and they magnify or describe normal experiences as negative just to feel more important or to get some attention.

If this kind of chatter annoys you, you must decide if there is enough about this friendship to make it worth sticking around. You can try mentioning that your friend is lucky that her problems are a result of so much talent, or point out the real health problems of a mutual friend, hoping that she will notice that by comparison, she is truly lucky. Unless you are close enough to this person to help her see that you feel she is whining about what others might see as her good fortune, her behavior is unlikely to change. She might not even realize that her complaints seem petty, and you are likely to continue to find her irritating.

If her constant negative spin on what you see as enviable makes you feel worse about your own life, though, or makes you want not to share your own experiences, at least part of the problem may be yours. You may be comparing your own children to this friend's, and if your kids don't quite measure up, your discomfort with their lack of star status may be the real source of your discomfort. Try to sort out if you just don't like the backhanded bragging of this friend, or if you actually are insecure about your own kids' accomplishments before you decide that you don't want to put much more effort into this friendship.

Life is too short to be caught up in creating of problems where there are none. Decide whether or not this friendship merits tolerating the complaining that you so dislike. Everyone has her quirks and odd behaviors; if she is endearing in other ways, look beyond the whining and enjoy the parts of her you like and admire. If being with her becomes increasingly unpleasant, limit the friendship to group events. You don't have to like everything about every person you befriend, but you don't have to be friends with people whom you actually dislike. And you don't need to feel bad if you just don't like certain parts of people. That's normal!

My friends don't have kids yet; most aren't even in long-term relationships. What's wrong with me that I just don't find them very interesting anymore?

Before she became a mother, Phoebe went out with a group of girl-friends on a regular basis. They talked about work, their romances, and the hottest new movies, and stayed out late and had a wonderful time. Since motherhood, though, Phoebe finds that her interests and her stamina have changed. Instead of loving being out with the girls and wanting to eke out extra time, she longed to go home, get into her PJs, and snuggle with her husband and kids. It wasn't that her friends were no longer interesting; her interests had changed.

Phoebe felt terrible that she no longer enjoyed those outings, too. But please don't be too hard on yourself or your friends. You have different priorities and interests than you used to, and different interests than your friends'. You are neither more nor less fascinating as a person since you've become a mom, and they are not more nor less charming and fun because they have not had kids. You are all just in different places in your lives right now, and as a result, how you want to socialize, and sometimes even with whom you want to socialize, may also be different.

Try not to fret about this. The real friends, the soul mates in your life, will remain your friends despite any differences in life choices and energy for late-night partying. You may discover that you have more to talk about with these old pals when you see them one-on-one; seeing your friends individually allows you to talk to each other about what really matters to each of you, to compare and contrast how your lives have changed. With a mother's schedule, lunch or an early dinner may be more conducive to keeping in touch without wearing you out, and will let you maintain some emotional closeness with the friends who really matter to you.

Those more superficial relationships, regardless of how much fun they were, may fade naturally. You may realize that what you had in common was more about what you did together than about who you each are as people. When you are in such a different place in your life than the friends with whom you used to just hang out or go wild, and you no longer want to do what they want to do, the friendship may have run its course. It's okay to let it go.

Continue to see the friends you enjoy, whether as a group or as individuals, as long as seeing them gives you pleasure. Don't assume that there's anything wrong with either you or them, and chalk up your decreased interest to just the way things happen sometimes. Friendships come and go. Closeness changes within even the best and longest, most enduring relationships, and nearly always, no one is at fault. You are entitled to want what you want from your friendships, and to accept your different needs as simply that.

Chapter Six

Mothers Who Work

Jane was sitting at her desk at work, trying to catch up on phone calls and emails that had piled up while she was out of town for a conference, when the school nurse called. Her eight-year-old son had fallen and badly cut his knee; the nurse thought he probably needed stitches. Jane looked at her computer screen, checked her calendar, and took a deep breath. "Are you telling me I need to come and get him?" The nurse hesitated a moment, and then kind of chuckled, and said, "Well, yes, that's why I'm calling. I cleaned it and bandaged it, but I think he needs to be seen by a doctor right away. How soon can you get here?" Jane sighed, turned off her computer, and told the nurse that she needed to cancel a meeting, but she'd be there as soon as she could. Reluctantly, Jane cancelled the rest of her afternoon, gathered what work she could to bring home with her, and went to take care of her son. She hated to admit it, but she was more upset about missing the chance to catch up on her work than she was about her son. And she felt guilty that she hadn't just dropped everything and run to get him.

Many working mothers have similar stories. Whether you work just to pay the bills or because you absolutely love your career, whether you work sixty hour weeks or six hours per week, there are times when you feel torn between the demands of the workplace and the needs of your family. Working moms I know often tell me that they think about home when they are work and they think about work when they are home. They want to do a good job both professionally and personally, but it's draining to try to do it all. And while they often feel lucky to be able to work while having a family, they are exhausted and frequently feel pulled in many directions.

I worked outside the home part-time for several years while my kids were little, and I got a lot of mileage out of that job. It allowed me to maintain a professional identity. It got me out of the house, gave me something to talk about besides my kids and my husband, and brought in a tiny bit of money. But it also brought with it concerns that any working parent occasionally encounters. What if my sitter can't come when I have to go to work? Can I take more vacation days? Do I need new clothes? Am I ruining my child's life by working? Is it terrible that I love my job? Why do I feel so much more competent at work than I do at home? Should I feel guilty that I don't miss my kids when I am at work?

While it is certainly an improvement that our society seems to be more accepting of a greater variety of choices women have about work and motherhood, sometimes it's the choices themselves that are difficult. My mother was raised to become a wife and mother; she had no internal conflict about whether she should pursue a career or stay at home and raise her kids. Women today, though, have so many more options, and although there are very strong opinions out there to support whatever choice you make, there are also people who will question or even criticize whatever path you choose. We know how important early childhood development is, yet we give very little respect to child-care workers. Working moms sometimes look down on stay-at-home moms, considering them somehow less intelligent, interesting, or ambitious, while stay-at-home moms sometimes criticize working moms for "abandoning" their children, allowing them to be raised by baby-sitters.

It's been my experience, and this is borne out by research, that children are not damaged by having working mothers. If the child care is good, then the children will do just fine. Children do not get confused about who is the mother and who is the baby-sitter, their learning is not impaired, and there are no long-lasting problems as a direct result of the mother working. Yet working definitely stresses the mother, as she attempts to be all things to everybody, and tries to feel okay about juggling her many roles.

This chapter is for mothers who consider themselves working mothers. It's not just for women who work full-time outside their homes, because I think that women who work at all, whether full or part time, inside or outside the home, for a paycheck or as a volunteer, or even as a student, unpaid artist, or unpublished writer, share some similar issues about balancing work with motherhood. Whether you work four hours a week or fifty, if you work at something that doesn't directly involve taking care of your family, and if you think of yourself as a working mom, then you are a working mom and there will be material in this chapter that is pertinent to you.

In addition to finding ways to come to terms with the frustrations common to many working mothers, I hope this chapter and the next, which focuses on stay-at-home moms, will increase acceptance and understanding of the various choices women make. Mothers can work and still be excellent mothers. Working moms need to become comfortable with the choices that they've made, and as a society we need to be more supportive. I just don't believe that there is one best way to balance career and motherhood. Every individual woman is entitled to respect and tolerance for making a choice about work that is best for her and for her family, and no one but that individual can really know what is best. I hope this chapter helps you become more comfortable with your choice, and if it doesn't, I hope it helps you to make a choice that will be a better fit.

I love my kids and I love my job. So why do I feel so bad about wanting to work?

I believe that some women feel that somehow they just aren't quite motherly enough, or good enough mothers, if they want to work instead of staying home full time with their kids. Even though women have worked outside the home for most of recorded history, we still hold on to the idea that loving mothers want to be ever-present and available to their children. Many women believe that a good mother is "supposed" to put her children first, above all other things in her life, regardless of her temperament or the financial needs of the family.

In addition, we have few models of mothers who work without ambivalence, exhaustion, or regret. Women in the workplace tend to keep their emotional conflicts about work and home to themselves, or at least share them only with other mothers or trusted friends, for fear of not appearing committed to their careers. Working mothers on television are often unrealistically able to leave work at a moment's notice to care for a skinned elbow or school crisis, or, in fact, are seen only in their workplace or only in their homes. Seldom do we get to know women who love both their jobs and their families and do both equally well.

Many of the mothers I've talked with describe never thoroughly understanding what it feels like to choose to work when you have children at home until they become mothers themselves. But it is perfectly reasonable to love your profession, to love your family, and to make the choice to work full time; your children need not be hurt by that decision. As long as working makes you happy, and you have good child care, your children will benefit. You want to show your kids that there are lots of ways to lead constructive, contented lives, and if working outside the home affords you the personal satisfaction you need, and your children are well cared for while you are working, then you are doing the right thing for you and your family.

If you and your husband are in agreement that your work is important to the well-being of the family and the kids are appropriately attended to, you have nothing to feel guilty about. Remember, guilt is about doing something you know you shouldn't, and working outside the home is absolutely acceptable. Children of working moms, especially those who love their work, do just fine. In fact, they may do even better because they grow up with an example of a mother who loves her children and her life. Give your children that, and you should feel proud.

I've read somewhere that a mom shouldn't work too many hours outside the home while her children are little. How many hours are too many?

These are the sorts of didactic remarks tossed off by so-called experts that make my skin crawl. There is no magic number under which you can relax, smug in the knowledge that you are doing everything right, or over which you must turn in your "I

Love My Mommy" T-shirts and mugs. The number of hours a woman "should" work outside the home depends on too many individual factors to be so easily determined. What's the right number for you and your family may be far too many or too few hours for somebody else.

Here's what you need to consider when you have young children and both parents work.

- Are your children well cared for when you are not with them?
- Do you feel that you're involved in the important aspects of your children's development?
- Are you comfortable with the number of hours you're working?
- Are your children comfortable with your work-home balance?
- Do you and your children feel good about each other most of the time?
- When you are home, are you able to focus on and care for your kids properly?
- Are your children doing well in general?

If you answered "yes" to the above questions, chances are that you are not working too many hours. Every woman and every family must find the balance of work and staying home that makes sense to them. And remember that just because someone doesn't work outside the home doesn't mean that she is spending more time with her kids. I've known several women who didn't "work," but who did so much volunteer work, exercising, or visiting with friends that they were with their children even fewer hours a week than some so-called working moms.

So find the balance of work and staying home that works for you and don't worry about the magic number. The number of hours you spend with your family matters much less than how you all feel about the situation. If you are content with your choice, your child-care arrangement works well, and you enjoy your children when you are with them, it will all be okay.

I work full-time outside the home, but I often worry that I am so tired when I am home that I'm just not emotionally available to my kids. How can I be a good worker and a caring, involved mom?

The emotional and physical demands of work leave lots of moms (and dads, too) drained and not as attentive or energetic as they'd like to be. Jill, a journalist, described fielding work-related phone calls at a little league softball game when she should have been cheering as her daughter caught fly balls in right field. Her body was at the game, but her mind was in the office. Katherine, a waitress, knows that her children look forward to her coming home every evening, to telling her all about their adventures; they expect her undivided attention, but often she all she wants is to eat a quick snack and put her feet up. The demands of work frequently seem to usurp so much energy—physical and emotional—that there is nothing left over for family at the end of the day.

Happily, I believe that you can be both a dedicated worker and a devoted mother. It doesn't always come easily, but if you have enough energy and support, know yourself and your abilities and limitations, and stay organized, you can be a great working mom. When you notice that your work is encroaching on your home life, take these steps.

Make sure you have enough physical and emotional energy.

- Take very good care of yourself. Eat healthfully, exercise regularly, even if that means you take the stairs instead of the elevator, and get enough sleep. When you are physically fit and well-rested, your emotionally availability should increase. Taking time to take care of yourself should not be seen as taking time away from family, as it will give you the extra energy you need to be an attentive and effective family member.
- Maintain contact with friends and activities that boost your spirits. Taking a few minutes a day to feed yourself emotionally by chatting with your best friend or pursuing enjoyable hobbies will give you the psychological sustenance you need to be able to turn around and give to your family.
- Nurture your marriage. Having two parents actively involved in the life of the family decreases the burden on each parent and creates solid bonds between all family members.

Make certain that you have enough support.

- Use your support system. For example, arrange for carpools for kids' activities. And say "yes" when friends offer to help you.
- Don't make yourself crazy trying to do what you aren't able to do, either for your family or others, but offer support whenever you can and ask for and accept support when you need it.
- Delegate tasks that don't need to be done specifically by you, both at work and at home. Too often moms think that they need to be doing everything when it's perfectly reasonable to

have your teenager take out the trash or your coworker file those papers.

⚜ Don't be embarrassed to ask for assistance when you need it. People often enjoy being able to help; it's a good way to connect.

⚜ Don't assume that because you are the mother you must do all the child care and housekeeping yourself. Share household chores with your husband, child-care provider, and your children (even a toddler can learn to put dirty laundry in the hamper).

Know yourself.

⚜ If you believe that your working prevents you from being the kind of mother you want to be, consider making some changes. Work a different job, change your hours, or go to part time.

⚜ If you love what you do, if working is what makes you *you*, then accept that you may need to adjust your ideas about what it means to be a good mother.

⚜ Some people simply need a period of time to make the mental transition from "worker" to "parent." If your mind is on the job, you won't focus on your family. Give yourself time at the end of each workday to unwind before you assume the Mommy role. Take a brief walk after work, read a book while commuting, or insist that you have time to change your clothes before the sitter goes home. Don't think of this as simply more time away from your family, but as insurance that when you are with your family, you are emotionally there.

⚜ Not all women are particularly emotionally nurturing. If you just don't find the daily routines of child care as interesting as your work, make certain that you find other meaningful ways to connect with your children. Share stories of your own childhood; develop activities that you each can enjoy. Take walks together or make Saturday morning brunch a ritual. Do laundry or cook together. You may not be as emotionally connected as you'd like but you can still build positive memories. Maybe as your children get older you'll find other ways to relate.

- If you realize that sitting on the floor, finger painting, or snuggling during thunderstorms with your kids is not for you, make sure that your children are getting adequately nurtured elsewhere. If Dad is the better listener, that's fantastic. If the baby-sitter can offer your children a more emotionally nurturing adult model, that's okay, too. Your job is to provide for your children's needs. No mother does everything well, so ensure that what you don't do well gets done by someone else.

Become better organized. I know this sounds like one more burden, but better organization often leads to more free time. When you are efficient and organized, things you have to do but don't especially enjoy doing get done more quickly, allowing you more hours for pleasurable activities.

- Set clear priorities and try to take care of essentials first.
- Do your grocery shopping less often; buy at least a week's supply of food at a time, and buy nonperishables in bulk.
- Prepare double quantities of freezable items (freezing portions for future use) so that you have to cook less often.
- Ask friends for tips on how they eliminate unnecessary chores.

- Hire a housekeeper if you can afford one.
- Never do less than a full load of laundry, and fold it all while watching a favorite TV show or talking to a friend on the phone.
- Get the kids to help with chores. This way you can talk to each other while setting the table and there's less for you to do by yourself.
- Schedule time for togetherness.

Spending time with your family is as important as work. Ideally, it should also be enjoyable. If you genuinely can't find a way to free up some time or if you have no real interest in your kids, you may need some more intensive emotional work. Seek a professional psychotherapist to help you work out what's preventing you from being closer to your kids.

You can be an excellent mother even if you aren't with your children as often as you'd like. It isn't the amount of time spent that matters but the closeness and caring that are evident when you are together. You can also be a good mother if you can recognize your limitations, whatever they are, and make sure that your children get what they need elsewhere.

My job is very demanding, so occasionally I can't make it to my kids' school plays or games. How can I keep my job and avoid all the guilt of missing parts of my kids' childhoods?

One of the hardest aspects of being a mother is finding a way to balance everything in your life. Not only are you a mother; you are a person who has many interests and responsibilities. Many parents feel bad when they can't attend all their children's activities. Some even change careers or choose to stay at home with their kids while they are very young because they prefer that to worrying about missing certain important events. It seems to me that the parents who feel worst about work intruding on family time are the ones who are most ambivalent about either their jobs or their relationships with their children. I truly believe that if you have made choices about work that are best for you and your family, for whatever reasons, then you don't need to feel guilty when occasionally you miss a child's activity. But just because you shouldn't feel guilty doesn't mean you won't.

Some jobs are simply not very conducive to being able to attend a class play or reliably get to after-school activities; if this describes your work situation, you and your children may have to learn to live with your missing a lot of daytime events. Some things may be out of your control; if this is the case for you, and your job is inflexible, explain this to your kids, and become involved with them in activities that meet when you aren't working.

If your employer or your specific job has some wiggle room, work toward maximizing your productivity and flexibility. Sometimes offering to switch schedules with a coworker or to come in to work when you aren't scheduled to make up for time when you'll go to your kids' activities, will be acceptable and make you more available to your children. And often, becoming better organized both at work and at home allows you to plan ahead so that work won't conflict with as many of your children's events.

If you feel that your children or your relationships with them are actually suffering from your frequent absences, then you might need to consider your options. Can you change your work schedule with advance notice? Can you use vacation or personal days (or half days) to chaperone the class field trip? Some work-places allow you to use sick days or vacation days at your own discretion. Can you work longer hours another day to compensate when you do take off for school conferences? Can you adjust your starting or ending time with advance notice? Sometimes work environments are friendlier than you think.

If you feel that your work frowns upon your taking time to attend to special family events, is it really the best place for you? If your attitudes about work and family aren't consistent with that of your workplace, it may ultimately be in your best interests to find another position with a more family-friendly environment. More and more companies are allowing and even encouraging flexible hours and supporting your commitments to family, as they have come to understand that a worker who feel less conflict is a better, more loyal worker. If your workplace isn't family friendly, consider finding one that is.

I stayed home when my first child was little, but after my second was born, I went back to work. How can I make it up to my second that I haven't been around as much for her?

As much as you might try, you will never be the same parent to the second child as you were to the first. But that isn't a bad thing. Each child will reap different benefits from your parenting. Your first may have had the advantage of your full attention at home, but your second has the experience of living with an older sibling, more experienced parents, and possibly a more contented and financially secure mom. No matter how hard you may try, you will never treat your children all the same, regardless of whether you work or not, and they will continue to have different experiences than each other.

Most families go through changes that make growing up different for each child. Kathy decided to be a stay-at-home mom when her first child, Mitch, was little, but she was offered the job of her dreams shortly after giving birth to her second child. She was thrilled to take it, but admits that she was around a whole lot more for Mitch than for the baby. But Kathy is philosophical about it. Each of her children has gotten something special from their relationships with their mother; Mitch had all that time with his mother in close attendance, but the baby has a role model who loves her job and is a happier person. Life changes, situations change, and families change along with them.

Your oldest would have had more time alone with you whether or not you'd returned to work simply by having been the only child around. It's nearly impossible for anyone to focus as much on any subsequent child. So the key factor here isn't really how much or little time you spend with your second compared to how much time you spent with your first; what's important is the quality of the time you do spend with each child and how good or guilty you are feeling about it. If you are ecstatic about working, if you feel better about yourself when you work, or if the added income increases your sense of fiscal comfort (and assuming you do spend some time together and have good child care) then your second child will enjoy growing up in a family in which the mother feels good about her life, regardless of how many hours you are away. When mom is content and child care is good, your children will all thrive.

However, if you believe that by working you've neglected your second child, your behavior will likely reflect that guilt. Although it's a rare child who counts how many hours his mother spends with each child and then uses that calculation to determine that he's being shortchanged, if *you* feel you're treating your kids unfairly, they will pick up on your feelings and believe it themselves. You want your children to feel loved and attended to, not to measure your love in hours or dollars spent.

If you really do love your children equally and you want to be working, then give yourself a break. The best parenting is not doing everything exactly the same for each child; it's loving each child and providing for his or her specific needs. If you are a caring, considerate, and involved mother, your second child won't suffer because you stayed home with her brother but not with her.

If you are still worried about the amount of time you spend with your kids, when you come home from work, spend time with your children, together and individually. Talk about their days and listen to what they want to tell you. Evaluate your parenting by the quality of the relationship you have with your children, not by anything quantifiable, and your children will learn to appreciate the time you spend together rather than resent the time you are apart.

My job requires me to travel, which I truly enjoy. I have great child-care arrangements, so why do I feel guilty whenever I have to be away from my family?

You feel guilty probably because you are enjoying something that you believe you shouldn't. Although you can easily admit that you enjoy traveling, it sounds like you believe that you *shouldn't* enjoy being away from your family.

This is one of those situations in which I believe it is valuable to truthfully assess what it is that makes you uncomfortable.

- Is your child-care arrangement really adequate? If you feel that when you travel, your friends, husband, or relatives are overextended trying to cover the child care while you are away, then your guilt may make some sense. If your child-care arrangement doesn't cover your traveling time, find another way to care for your children while you are away. Then you can leave knowing that both your kids and their caregiver will be content with the situation.

- Does your travel schedule require you to miss too many significant events in your kids' lives? Maybe you need to rethink your job, as it may not be the travel that makes you feel bad, but the sheer number of hours you are required to be away in general.

- Are your kids doing just fine, when you wish they missed you a bit more? Then you need to adjust your thinking a bit and become more comfortable with being a working/traveling mom.

- Are your kids, recognizing your ambivalence toward traveling; manipulating you or trying to get you to loosen bedtimes or bring them lots of gifts to assuage your guilt? If so, your guilt is teaching your children to be manipulative, and that benefits only the hotel and airport gift shops.

- Do you feel guilty that when you go away, you are able to enjoy adult activities, uninterrupted sleep, and forget the more mundane sides of parenthood?

- Do you feel guilty because you don't miss your kids?

Many traveling moms and dads hesitate to admit how much they enjoy being away, assuming that they must be very bad parents if they like the enforced separation from their families. Yet lots of moms and dads who must travel away from home for their jobs realize that being away from home isn't all bad, and often that's the real source of guilt.

It's perfectly okay to enjoy your occasional independence from your family. If your children are well cared for while you are gone, if no one is especially overwhelmed by your absence, if you don't allow your guilt to lead to spoiling your children or being manipulated by them, then go ahead and travel, and leave the guilt as well as the kids at home. Work-related travel can help your job and your family if you allow yourself to enjoy the break and come home refreshed. If there are problems in your work-travel-home situation, solve them, but otherwise accept that you enjoy the respite that work-related trips provide, be a great parent when you are at home, and relax.

I stayed at home when my children were very little. Now that they are both in school, I've gone back to work full time. How can I come to terms with the fact that my going back to work requires everyone to do so much more around the house?

Every family handles household chores differently. Some parents expect their children to be responsible for various tasks at a very early age, increasing the level of responsibility as the child matures, while others demand very little, doing nearly all the housework, cooking, cleaning, and organizing themselves. It sounds like you went from being a stay-at-home mom who did the bulk of the household and family-related work, to being a working-outside-the-home mom who needs to share it. Although objectively, dividing household tasks equitably makes sense, emotionally, you feel like you're shirking your duties. Your struggle isn't just that the rest of your family has to work harder now; it's that you are the cause of the change of rules.

Sometimes the best way to solve a problem is to redefine it. You are working full time, which means you are less available to take care of the house, do the laundry, cooking, and carpooling. If you believe that taking care of those things *should* be your responsibility, then it makes sense that you feel as if you are dumping your load onto the shoulders of your husband and kids. Then the problem isn't really that your family has to pitch in more; it's that you feel guilty that you are no longer the one doing everything.

Being a Supermom, or even a very good mom, does not require you to be the one doing everything, and your family may actually benefit from being more involved in the home. By taking over some of the jobs you used to do, your husband and children will develop an understanding of all it takes to run a household. In addition to appreciating you and how much you did for them before you went back to work, they will become more proficient at taking care of themselves. Children who help around the house are better prepared for life on their own, and contributing to the family's well-being may boost their self-esteem. Having family members do some of the chores will not diminish your standing as a great mom. Really.

As a stay-at-home mom, you undoubtedly felt that you offered your family certain important services. Now that you are working outside the home, you are still doing good things for your family; they are just different. Your working shows your kids that good mothers can work outside the home, augment the family income, and derive satisfaction from the workplace. It also shows them that you have interests and talents beyond being their caretaker. Trusting them to chip in more shows that you have confidence in them.

Your family will adjust to the changed division of labor most easily if you can come to terms with it yourself. If working is important to you, whether for the financial or personal comforts it gives, you have no need for guilt. If you are doing what is right for you and your children are being cared for appropriately, relax. Assign jobs according to the abilities and time availability of each family member, reassess what absolutely must be done, when it needs to be done, and by whom, and be patient. You and your family will all adjust to this change.

How can I tell my sitter what to do with the kids when I'm not always sure myself?

When a new mom hires an experienced child-care provider, both the mother and the sitter may wonder who really is the authority. If you've never been an employer before, and if you are a relatively new mother, it can feel very peculiar to be in a position to tell your nanny or day-care provider how you want things done. But just because she has more experience caring for children doesn't mean that your ideas about taking care of *your* children are any less valid than hers.

Lots of moms experience similar awkwardness when it comes to telling a sitter what to do. You've read lots of parenting books and you know your specific children, yet she has changed more diapers and played in the park with more kids than you can imagine. So you feel a bit sheepish demanding or suggesting that she do things differently just because you want her to, and while you want things done your way, you aren't necessarily sure what way that actually means.

Start by making sure that you feel comfortable with your

child-care arrangement. Check references and trust your gut feelings about potential caregivers, and do not use anyone who intimidates you. Spend time with your caregiver and your child, get to know her as a person—because the person she is, her tastes, interests, and attitude, will impact your family. Be clear from the beginning what kinds of things you want to hear about at the end of each work day, what situations you want her to handle without your input, and which circumstances require a call to Mom or Dad. If you have a caregiver that you and your kids are comfortable with, then talking with her about how to handle your family should come naturally.

Of course, it is normal to disagree with your caregiver on occasion, whether or not she is vastly more experienced with children than you are, because there are lots of perfectly reasonable and acceptable ways to raise children. You must be able to work with your sitter, discuss your individual ideas and styles of managing day-to-day living. If your nanny isn't receptive to your requests, then she isn't the best child-care provider for you. Good child-care providers expect moms to have different opinions and approaches and are willing to talk with you to come to an agreement.

If your child-care provider is really great, talking with her about why she does certain things differently than you do could be tremendously enriching for you and your family. However, if, in addition to feeling that she is wonderful and that you are lucky to have her, you still feel bad telling her what to do, *tell her that*! Try saying, "Overall, you're really spectacular, and I feel kind of uncomfortable saying this, but I'd really prefer that you put Michael to nap in his crib, not let him fall asleep in his stroller." This gets the message across with a minimum of weirdness. And try to remind yourself that she may have lots of experience, but this is your family, and you are entitled to have things done your wa

I feel guilty because my child cries whenever I leave for work. What should I do?

Children cry when their mommies leave them with a baby-sitter or at day care for a variety of reasons. Some children have more trouble with separation than others; at certain stages of development, children become more aware of the mother as a separate being and cry out of discomfort about the separation; and some cry because crying gets the mommy to delay leaving or lavish gifts and attention on the child. Rarely is the crying an indicator of something more serious. You may feel better about your child's reaction if you knew whether or not the crying is age appropriate, and she'll soon outgrow it; if it is manipulative, and you need to respond differently; or if there is something more concerning going on.

Ask yourself the following questions:

- Is this a new behavior?
- Does your child settle down once you are totally out of view or earshot?
- Does your child cry when you leave him in other situations, such as with your husband or when you aren't going to work?
- When your child cries, do you always come back to him and spend more time with him before heading off to work?
- Since he's begun to cry when you leave, have you brought gifts home from work for him or spent more time with him when you are at home?
- Does your child seem peaceful and content once he's adjusted to your leaving? (You can ask your sitter, but you can also verify this by making telephone calls during the day, and to

listen for crying, asking a friend to stop by and check, or making surprise visits.)

- ❧ Does your child seem calm and cheerful when you return to him?
- ❧ Do you notice any other problems besides the increased crying when you leave?
- ❧ Does your child still eat and sleep normally?
- ❧ Are there unexplained marks, scrapes, or bruises on your child's body?

What you need to do is determine the cause of the crying. If the tears are a normal part of your child's development, there is no problem. If the tears are excessive, or if there is undue discord with the child-care provider, you need to know that.

Many children, if not all, go through what is commonly called separation anxiety; this occurs most often toward the end of the first year of life or early in the second year. Lots of children also experience separation issues at later points in life, especially around the beginnings of new experiences or family stress or illnesses. These are also normal, as long as the anxiety or tears resolve relatively quickly and the child is able to calm down and resume normal activities and attitudes shortly after you leave. If your child is experiencing this normal and age-appropriate separation anxiety, he might also cry when you leave him with his dad or any other familiar person. It's a stage that is sometimes heartbreaking for you, but it's a normal part of the developmental process of your child, which indicates that he is beginning to understand that he is a unique and separate individual from you. *These tears are not at all related to your working.*

Most of the time, children who sob when their mothers leave them for work stop crying as soon as mom is out of sight or hearing, and mom stays upset far longer than the child does. Make sure that the child-care situation is safe and loving, and then accept that some tears are just a part of the normal process of saying good-bye. If you react too strongly to his tears, you might end up prolonging the situation. Your child will be able to sense that he has upset you, too, and your discomfort or guilt about leaving him might then contribute to his reaction when you leave. Similarly, if you respond to his crying by cuddling him more, coddling him, or otherwise feeling guilty and then indulging him inappropriately, he'll learn that he can manipulate you with tears. Once you have determined that he is really okay, that his child-care situation is safe and loving, don't allow his temporary distress to fuel your guilt. Leave him with a casual and loving kiss, and go to work.

If your child is constantly in distress or if you both struggle with the separation, there may be other problems you need to face. Maybe you really don't want to be working, so you focus on your child's discomfort as a reason to quit. Perhaps you love work so much that you feel particularly guilty that you don't want to stay at home. Perhaps separations are still hard for you, too. If the tears continue for an extended period of time—both in terms of how long your child cries each workday and for how many weeks this behavior continues (more than several weeks)—or if the child seems truly inconsolable, you might find it worth your while to check it out with a health care professional. If there's a problem, you can solve it, and if not, you'll have the peace of mind of knowing that this is just part of your child's "normal" experience.

Regardless of the source of the tears, bear in mind that many mothers feel the same misgivings you feel when you leave your child to go to work. Your child may be crying more or longer in part as a reaction to your ambivalence about working (or at least about leaving her). Remember that as long as the child care is good, your working will have no direct negative impact on your child; there is no cause for guilt. Accept that separations are difficult, but also accept that this doesn't mean you should not work outside your home.

Leave your child with a hug, a kiss, and a firm assurance that you love her and will be back later. Then go to work and get on with your day.

I have a wonderful child-care provider, but as much as I hate to admit it, I'm jealous of her! What's wrong with me?

There's probably nothing wrong with you at all. Most moms who work occasionally feel those nasty twinges of jealousy toward their nannies or baby-sitters at one time or another. Although jealousy is an uncomfortable feeling, it's sometimes an occupational hazard of the working mom.

Here's the dilemma: you want your children to have the best child care imaginable while you work, you want your children and your provider to grow to love each other, and you know that your baby-sitter and kids will share experiences in which you will not take part. Knowing that your children and their caregiver have a wonderful relationship actually comforts you and allows you to focus fully on your work when you are there. While objectively you truly want your children to feel close to the person who takes care of them when you can't, seeing that love—or hearing about the fun they have together—may make you feel left out. That's when the jealousy pops up, unwelcome, annoying, and not at all unusual.

I think there are two common sources of jealousy. Emma,

mother of six-month-old Jack, worries that their nanny will somehow replace her. She's terrified that her son will think their sitter is his mother, or worse still, prefer the sitter to her. Beth, a mother of twins, laments that her child-care provider gets to experience things with her kids that she will miss. The first fear is understandable, but highly unlikely to prove true, while the second concern is more realistic.

As much as you may fear that they won't, your children will always know who is who. Studies have shown that no matter how many hours a day your child spends in day care, he or she will know which one of you is mom, and which is the caregiver. Kids will have a different relationship with you than they have with the baby-sitter.

If your relationship with your kids is solid, if you spend time together when you are home and enjoy each other's company when you do, and if you feel both loving toward and loved by them, then their closeness to the sitter is a bonus. I don't know of any children who were hurt by loving or being loved by too many people. Instead of succumbing to those jealous feelings, pat yourself on the back for providing your kids with such excellent care.

However, if you feel that your relationship with your kids is strained, if your jealousy rises because the kids seem more relaxed and happy with the sitter than with you, then some help might be in order. Ask yourself the following questions:

- Are you spending so much time at work that you are rarely with your kids?
- Are you too tired or stressed to connect emotionally with your kids when you are home?
- Do you show interest in your children, spend time genuinely listening to them and playing with them, when you can?

🕮 Are you crabby when you're home?

If your behavior *causes* your children to prefer the sitter, then please don't be jealous of the sitter; learn from her. Examine your relationship with your children. When you are with your kids, really be with them. If you travel, or work late, call them. When you are home, ignore all work or chores for half an hour each evening and play with your kids. Ask them about their day; put aside your own concerns and listen to theirs. Be grateful that your children have a loving presence in their lives, and try to feel and express more love for your kids yourself.

If you continue to be jealous, seek professional help. While it's highly unusual for kids to prefer their sitter to their mother, it occurs most often when the mother isn't emotionally connected to the children. And whatever you do, unless you have clear evidence that your sitter is somehow sabotaging your relationship with your kids, *do not fire the sitter.* Kids need the stability of loving child care; the last thing your children need is to lose a caring adult because you are jealous. If your relationship with your kids improves, you won't feel jealous anymore, which is what you all want anyway.

Interestingly, Grace, an attorney who works long hours, told me that her definition of a great nanny is one who doesn't tell you when little Seth turned over for the first time; she lets you discover his "new" skill yourself. The realities of your work may occasionally mean that your day-care provider will see Julia's first steps, or attend more of Mark's soccer games. Although jealousy that your caregiver may witness some of your children's firsts may be understandable, it is neither pleasant nor constructive. If you want or need to work outside the home, and you have great child care, your children will have someone loving to cheer them on whether you are at work or not. That is a great gift to give yourself and your family, and considered in those terms, you'll feel less of a sting when the cheerleader can't be you.

Ultimately, you must come to terms with the choices you have made. You can't be in two or three places at once, and that may sometimes result in your sitter being with your children when you wish you could. If you feel jealous more often than not, or your job takes you away from your kids more than you can tolerate, maybe you need to rethink your work situation. Even if your work–home balance fit you perfectly six months ago, reexamine how it suits you now. Be honest with yourself and your family, and then you can be grateful, rather than resentful, that your kids have such wonderful child care.

I can't concentrate on my job. How can I stop thinking about my kids so much when I'm at work?

Something in your work–home balance may not be right for you. While it's not uncommon for a working mom to think about her kids when she should be focusing on her job, if you find that you are constantly distracted, it is likely that you feel that there is something wrong with either your work or your child-care situation. Thinking about your kids when you should be concentrating on your job may reflect either trouble at work or trouble at home. You can't fix the trouble, though, until you've identified it. Ask yourself the following:

- Are you working more or different hours than you want to work?
- Does your job demand you to work at unpredictable times,

often with little advance notice?

- Are you unhappy with the job itself?
- Do you get paid enough to cover costs incurred by working (like child care or dry-cleaning)?
- Do you feel unappreciated at work or at home?
- Do you feel that your child-care arrangement is inadequate?
- Are your kids or your husband asking you to quit working?
- Have your children's behaviors recently changed significantly?
- Would you rather just be at home?
- Are you sleep-deprived?

If it is your work arrangement that is bothering you, you may need to make some changes.

- Talk to your boss to see if you can work more agreeable hours. Sometimes a simple schedule change will allow you more time with your kids while they're awake so that they won't be on your mind so much at work.
- Explain your need to know your schedule in advance whenever possible. Some people, maybe you, become more anxious when they can't plan ahead.
- If it's the job itself you don't like, start looking for other options. Maybe it's time to change jobs or even careers.
- If your income from work barely covers the costs of working, if you are concerned that your children are suffering, or if you just don't enjoy your job, working may not be right for you now. Consider cutting costs at home (eliminate a housekeeper, start shopping at discount stores more often) so that you can stay at home until you find something either more lucrative or more enjoyable.
- If you feel unappreciated either at work or at home, noth-

ing will feel right. Sometimes when women are especially efficient, people forget to tell them how great they are; just because you aren't hearing it doesn't mean that those around you don't appreciate you. Tell your boss, coworkers, or family how you feel and ask for clearer expressions of approval.

- If your family doesn't support your working, even the least ambivalent person can start to feel bad. Talk to your family; let them know that you understand they would rather you be at home, but that your working is important to you and to your family. Reassure them that you love them and think about them, and make sure you understand their resistance to your working. Help each other become supportive of each family member's choices.

- If you truly would rather be a stay-at-home mom, find a way to do that. Try working from home, work fewer hours, or work when your husband is at home. Cut back on expenses or move to a smaller home, if necessary. Not everyone who thinks she should work really *wants* to work. Sometimes you just aren't ready to be in the workforce, and most of the time, families can do better than they think on only one income.

- If you aren't getting enough sleep, concentration will be hard to achieve. Take better care of yourself, eat properly, and rest on your lunch breaks.

If your work situation itself is perfectly fine, your family supports you working, yet you are still distracted at work, think about your child care. Worrying that your kids aren't well cared for is enough to distract anybody. If you have real doubts as to the reliability or adequacy of your child-care arrangement, *make changes*. Hire someone new, ask a friend to step in until you find a better replacement, or take a leave of absence from work if you must. Don't leave your kids with someone you don't trust.

If you can sort out why you're so distracted at work, you can fix the problem. Be willing to be honest with yourself, your employer, and your family and make changes when necessary. When you feel good about your work, family situation, and your child care, you will regain your ability to concentrate and be fully functional wherever you are.

Is it silly to go back to work just to maintain a bit more equality and balance in our marriage?

People work for many reasons, not all of them financial. Of course many women do work to help support their families, but some mothers work because they love their jobs, some don't enjoy being stay-at-home moms, some work to advance in their careers more rapidly, some want to be role models for younger women, some want daily contact with peers, and some work because they believe it strengthens their marriages. Whatever makes sense for you is okay.

While I believe that mothers should be able to work if they want to for *whatever* reason, working to regain some equality in your marriage may or may not solve your problem. Equality in a marriage is a hard thing to define and sometimes hard to achieve. If you both measure your contributions to the family in terms of income, then going back to work may be the best way to regain some equality. But if you assess contributions according to everything else that a family needs, including cooking, cleaning, attending school events, carpooling, hugging, playing, and listening, you may come up with a different accounting to how much you each do.

Victoria and Gary strive for an equal marriage, but found themselves wondering what that really meant once they had kids. Gary earned significantly more than Victoria ever could in their current careers, and Victoria loved staying at home. When they examined carefully what each of them did to keep the family functioning and content, it became clear that they were each very busy. Although Gary brought home almost all of the family income, Victoria did most of the housework, cooking, and child care. Maybe these are sex-stereotyped roles, but they were roles each enjoyed, and the family functioned well. They agreed that while their relationship was perhaps not *measurably* equal, they both felt it was equitable.

However, if you and/or your husband measure the equality in your marriage by how much money you each deposit in your joint account, then going back to work may be just what you need, particularly if it's you who feels that your contributions are lacking. What's important here is not the decision to work or not to work, but what it means to you and your husband to be a full participant in your marriage. As long as you are both comfortable with the choice, it is a good choice.

Just be sure that your decision to work addresses the actual problem in the balance in your marriage. What's important to figure out is how both you and your husband can feel emotionally fulfilled, supported, appreciated, valued, and financially secure. How that balance is achieved is much less important than that you both feel satisfied that it has.

I'm being offered a position in which I could work from my home. How can I know I'll like that?

Some women thrive on working from home, while others find it increases stress. There are several things to consider when you try to decide whether or not working from home is right for you.

- Does your home have an appropriate space in which you will be able to work? Depending on the work you do, you are likely to need a room in which you can remain undisturbed and isolated from the activity of other family members, and in which you have enough space and appropriate wiring for whatever equipment you need. If you have a small home, or if you will be using the telephone a lot, you may need to think about soundproofing, also.
- Can your workspace adapt to your changing needs? Will you be able to see clients or add equipment at a later date if the need arises?
- Will you be able to concentrate on your work while at home? Some moms, comforted that they can get to their children in an instant should the need come up, enjoy being nearby, while others find themselves too easily distracted, listening for their kids, or escaping work to watch TV or do the laundry.
- Will your child-care arrangement be conducive to your working from home? If your children will be at home while you are working, can your sitter ensure that you will remain undisturbed, or will she be likely to allow your children to interrupt you while you work? Nannies need to be both firm and creative when Mom is physically in the home but unavailable.

- Will you miss seeing coworkers on a regular basis? When you work from home, there are limited opportunities for socializing with colleagues.
- Are you disciplined enough to work without on-site supervision? Will you be as productive as you need and want to be?
- Will you miss dressing up and getting away from your house?

If, after thinking about these issues, you still think working at home will be good for you, then do it. Most families adapt well to whatever set-up makes Mom happy, and many moms thoroughly enjoy working in their pajamas, just steps away from the other comforts of home.

How can I convince my husband that my working outside the home won't compromise my ability to be a good wife and mother?

You need to clarify, both to yourself and to your husband, exactly what it means to be a good wife and mother; once you've done that, you are most of the way there. If your husband and you believe that you should be home whenever the kids are home, sew and cook daily, do the carpooling, grocery shopping, laundry, and cleaning, help the kids with their homework, and have energy left over at the end of the day to rub Hubby's feet, it may be hard to convince him that you can hold down a job and graciously do everything else he expects of you. On the other hand, if being a good mother and wife means that you make sure that your family's needs are being met, whether by you or by some other loving and trustworthy person, you stand a good chance of accepting that your working won't detract from the family well-being.

Working does not have to limit your maternal and wifely value or skill, so don't even entertain the idea that it could. Instead of dwelling on how working might detract from your domestic roles, figure out what you and your husband each need in your lives to be happy and who should provide it. How good you are at family life or how content your loved ones are overall is not determined by whether or not you, the mom, work outside the home. Much more important is how you and your husband work together to take care of all the family needs.

I tend to believe that people should, whenever possible, do what they want to do and that women who choose to work outside the home are just as good wives and mothers as women who choose to stay at home. In fact, women who are working outside the home because they *want* to are often better mothers and wives than they would be if they stayed at home because they are doing what feels right to them. They are more content and satisfied than they would be if they gave work up, especially if they are staying at home because their husbands want them to or they think they *should*. If you stay home because your husband wants you there, even though you'd rather be working, you might not be as pleasant or efficient as either of you would hope.

Talk with your husband about both the needs of the family and your individual needs. One of the hardest tasks of family life is balancing the requirements and desires of each individual with those of the family as a unit. Try to decide together how best to achieve that balance for your family so that whatever your decision about work, you both are comfortable with it. Many, many mothers work and maintain a happy and well-adjusted family life, but it's a lot harder if you and your husband aren't both supportive of your working.

If you can't come to a mutual understanding about your working outside the home, get counseling. You and your husband are both entitled to feel good about how you take care of your family, and no one should either have to work or to stay at home against her will. You and your mate both need to feel comfortable that regardless of whether you work or not, all family needs are being met, and all family members are reasonably content with how that is accomplished.

I work part time. Will I have the same opportunities for career advancement?

I'd like to be able to say "yes" unequivocally, but it's not so simple. Some careers and some employers are more accepting and willing to be flexible than others. On a positive note, in my years working with new mothers about family issues, I have seen vast improvement and greater creativity and acceptance of a variety of paths toward career success. More and more women are working part time or flexible hours, job sharing, or working from home. Some employers welcome part timers into their companies, knowing that they are often more dedicated, productive, and efficient than their full-time counterparts. However, some professions and some specific employers are less willing to consider part-time employment as ready for the fast track.

Check with other employees in your current or most recent job. If your profession has a union or national organization, inquire with them. Different industries are more or less tolerant of working mothers or of women who take time off or work part time. For example, it used to be that women attorneys seemed to have to choose either to give up their jobs altogether when they became mothers, or if they worked, they had to continue to work (very) full time. While that is still the case more often than not, some law firms are beginning to be more respectful of and responsive to women employees who want to be more available to their families. Find a company that values and encourages part-time workers.

Your ability to move ahead in your job is generally determined by your dedication, ability, experience, and hard work. If you are very clear about your limits and extremely efficient and focused while you are at work, your employer will know and appreciate your contributions.

- When you are at work, be fully at work. When there is a conflict, face it directly and quickly so that your work is not compromised.
- Come in for staff meetings and be willing to take important or crisis calls from home, even on your off days, if possible.
- Have a realistic game plan for when you might return to full-time employment.
- Have excellent and reliable child care, ideally with a back-up plan so that if someone gets sick, you can still get to work.
- Do not allow calls from your kids (or call home yourself) while you are at work, except in an emergency.

Although many more mothers are working, and working when their children are younger, there are countless paths your particular career may take; try your best to do what you want to do. Do your research about your particular position and professional goals and make an educated choice that feels right. Don't work full time just to prove your commitment to your job if working full time will make you miserable. This is you life, and as far as we know, it is likely to be the only one you get. Do the kind of work you want to be doing now, keeping your professional plans in the back of your mind. Although it's good to be thinking about your future, make sure that you are happy now, too.

Chapter Seven

Mothers Who Stay at Home

Brianna, the mother of two young children, had recently moved to the suburbs. As she returned home from work one afternoon, a neighbor stopped by to introduce herself. Her neighbor, Emily, had two sons who were just a few months younger than Brianna's. Brianna was carrying her briefcase, and it was clear that she was returning from work, so Emily asked her what she did. Brianna told her a bit about her job, and then asked Emily the same question. Emily answered with a list a mile long: she sang in her church's choir; she volunteered at the local women's shelter; and she was on her preschool's planning committee. She was active in everything the community had to offer. Not once did she say that she was a stay-at-home mom—which she was.

Emily, faced with meeting a mother who worked outside the home, couldn't bring herself to say that she was a stay-at-home mom. She felt that she had to embellish her description of her life; she had to "keep up" with Brianna-with-the-briefcase. I find it interesting how often stay-at-home moms are uncomfortable telling working moms that they stay at home. Even though they may be fiercely proud of having chosen to stay home while their children are young, they seem to harbor some embarrassment or fear that they won't be taken seriously by working moms.

Many stay-at-home moms I know, when asked that dreaded question "What do you do?" answer sheepishly, "I'm just a mom." *No one* is "just a mom" in my mind; being a mom is very hard work, and being a stay-at-home mom is a very important endeavor. Sadly, it seems to be undervalued not only by many people in our society, but also often by the stay-at-home moms themselves.

When moms spend most of their time at home with their kids, they have certain common concerns. While many women feel very fortunate to be able to stay at home with their children, and while they usually have chosen to stay at home because they believe that is the best arrangement for their children, stay-at-home mothers also often feel lonely, bored, unappreciated, and isolated. They love their children and the freedom to plan their days, but they also feel trapped and at the mercy of very demanding small people. They wonder if they are wasting their brains or advanced degrees spending so much time carpooling, and they receive little respect.

Even if you stay at home only a few days a week, there are issues that you face that may never have occurred to you before. You may question your dedication to your career. You may wonder about how to raise your children to believe in the equality of the sexes when the chores in your home seem to be divided sharply along gender lines. You may feel less important than your mate. You may feel less entitled to spend money if you aren't bringing in a paycheck. You may miss getting dressed up or the company of coworkers. You may feel that you've lost (at least temporarily) your former identity as an independent woman. And you may be treated shabbily by unenlightened employed people.

You don't need to be dissatisfied with your choice to stay at home to find yourself grappling with some of these concerns. Even when you know that staying home with your kids is exactly what you want to do, you may find certain aspects of this lifestyle dull or unappealing, and often, you may find other people's attitudes toward you downright rude. Staying home with the kids, even when staying home is clearly your best decision, does not come without its own share of difficult or aggravating elements.

I believe that there are many excellent routes to being a great mother, and staying home with your kids is certainly one of them. If you have the temperament and the financial ability to do so, staying home with your kids allows you to be a first-hand observer of your kids' big milestones, and lots of small, but meaningful, moments. Being there when they arrive home from school each day affords a direct and intimate involvement in your children's lives. Many stay-at-home moms cherish the opportunity to let chores slide and go outside on a gorgeous fall day, to watch icicles melt with an astonished toddler, to let the child's pace or the whims of the day direct their activities. Many, many pleasures exist for a stay-at-home mom, if she can just take the time to enjoy them.

Of course, on a miserable day, when the weather is brutal, the dirty laundry seems never-ending, the children are sick of each other and you, and you haven't spoken to a nonparenting adult in more than a week, those lovely moments may be quickly forgotten. All that freedom and fluidity can be uncomfortable for those who like more structure in their lives, it feels terrible to be treated as if you have only half a brain, and never receiving a paycheck or praise for your work can make you question your choice to stay at home. So stay-at-home moms feel bad a lot of the time, too.

Knowing that you're doing what's right for you helps a lot, but sometimes you need a little extra reassurance. This chapter provides that comfort. Stay-at-home moms (and this chapter also includes issues that concern *mostly*-stay-at-home moms—those moms who work outside the home part time) need to come to terms with these conflicted feelings. They need to tolerate and perhaps embrace the endless days and nights and the child-centered shift their lives have taken.

Stay-at-home moms appreciate being able to stay home, yet they feel guilty if they don't enjoy every minute. They love their freedom and miss having clear beginnings and endings to their tasks. They feel they are doing the most important, rewarding work imaginable, yet they feel unacknowledged and unrewarded. And all of these unexpected, conflicting emotions are normal. This chapter faces these feelings honestly, recognizes the universality of the conflicts, and helps stay-at-home moms learn to accept their chosen path—or realize if it isn't for them after all.

Why do I feel so bad when people seem condescending or unsupportive of my decision to be a stay-at-home mom?

Even when you feel comfortable with your life choices, it's insulting at worst, and unsettling at best, when others challenge or criticize your decisions. Although there has been tremendous progress in societal tolerance for women choosing their own individual paths in life, some people assume that a woman who chooses to stay at home with her kids must not be very career-oriented, liberated, or bright—or maybe all three. You and I know that many extremely capable and talented women want to be stay-at-home mothers, caring for their children day in and day out, and that the choice to stay at home reflects a person's values and temperament. It does not reflect their value as a worker, their intelligence, independence, or the degree of their feminism.

As you know, choosing to stay at home to raise your kids is not a decision most women make lightly. Even when staying at home seems the obvious best choice for you, many women still have some ambivalence about deciding to stay home; having others treat you condescendingly or challenge your choice puts you on the defensive. And being on the defensive may make you wonder if you have really made the right choice at all.

Although I've seen some decrease in the war between the stay-at-home and the working-outside-the-home moms over the last twenty years, there are still minor battles being fought. People have a hard time maintaining enough confidence in their own decisions not to be threatened by a friend or colleague making an opposing choice. That's what often causes working moms (who might silently wonder if they are hurting their children by working so much) to criticize you for "wasting" your education and intelligence by staying home with your kids, or the stay-at-home moms (who might secretly miss their professional lives) to chastise the working moms for "abandoning" their children. When women are comfortable and confident that the choices they've made are the best choices for them under their current circumstances, such offensive remarks and attitudes rarely occur.

If your so-called friends continue to put you on the defensive, please find other friends. Friends do not try to sway their friends to act in lockstep with each other. They are not threatened when you do things a little differently. Real friends want what is best for you and accept that you will often make different choices than each other.

Do your best to ignore the ignoramuses who try to make you feel bad for living your life and mothering your children the way you see fit. Your choice to stay at home is just that: your choice. It is neither better nor worse, in a broad sense, than working full time. When you feel at peace that being a stay-at-home mom is right for you, their comments may sting but not hurt quite so much. And your confidence will not be shaken.

Each family and each individual must find the balance that works. Working moms and stay-at-home moms have a lot in common in that they each want to provide for their families in the best, most comfortable way that they can. Do not feel bad that you are able to choose to stay at home, and don't try to make mothers who choose differently feel bad, either. If we could all realize that some moms are financially and temperamentally suited to stay at home with their kids while others are not, we would all feel a lot better.

Am I wasting my education by choosing to be a stay-at-home mom?

I don't believe that your education is lost when you become a stay-at-home mom; all the many aspects of your education and all other previous life experiences enrich you as a person and therefore enrich your mothering. Whatever your educational background, as a mother you will use your ability to think and analyze, to organize and interpret, and to consider how best to tackle problems or manage time. You may not be working in the field you for which you were trained, but your education is never wasted.

Of course, that doesn't prevent other people from telling you that you have wasted it, or you yourself from feeling that somehow all those semesters taking notes and studying for tests aren't useful now that you're a stay-at-home mom. But if you think about it for a minute, you may realize how pertinent your education was. While rarely does training to be a doctor, hairstylist, dog groomer, or history professor directly prepare you for motherhood, your education is probably more valuable than you realized.

Your education, no matter what field, prepared you for life. You learned to be disciplined, or to suffer the consequences if you are not, to think things through critically, to have a more open and facile mind, to be creative and efficient, and to have fun while you're at it. You learned how to respond differently to different teachers' demands, manage deadlines and stress, and budget both time and money. These are all extremely valuable skills for motherhood, as you must manage your home and children in a similar fashion. Yes, as a stay-at-home mom you take care of household tasks and children, but doing so involves not just the mechanics of housekeeping and child care, but also managing your time and helping your children develop into kind and capable human beings.

If you ask me, every bit of your education will stand you in good stead as you stay at home to help your children grow up successfully. And your children and husband, as well as you, will be glad that they have an educated, thoughtful woman there to help them grow. Don't worry when that nasty comment comes up, as it inevitably will. An education is hardly wasted when you are using everything you've ever learned to be a great wife and mother to your family.

I told my boss I'd come back to work after my maternity leave was over, but now that I have my baby, I want to stay at home. If that's best for me, why do I feel guilty?

You feel guilty because you made a commitment that you no longer want to keep. While you may feel some legitimate twinges of guilt if your decision to stay at home leaves your boss in a bind, you are not at all alone in having been unable to predict how you would feel once you had your baby. Many, many women experience similar changes of heart about this, including me. I was absolutely certain that I would return to work full time once my maternity leave was over, but as the days drew nearer and nearer, it became very clear that I did not want to return to work for more than a few hours a week. And I know lots of women who have the opposite response: early certainty that they'd want to stay home was followed by changing their minds, wanting to return to work as soon as they were back on their feet after delivery.

Schedule an appointment with your employer as soon as your decision to stay home is clear, and discuss your feelings with him or her face-to-face—without your baby in tow. When meeting with your boss, be direct, firm, and honest. To assuage your guilt, you can do a couple of things:

- If you have child care available, and are willing to return to work while they search for your replacement, offer to do so.
- If you would be willing to work part time or from home, suggest that. But be clear about your limits (number of hours or days per week) and do not agree to work more than you feel comfortable working.
- Offer to help train your replacement or to write comprehensive notes about your specific responsibilities, if you are able.
- Maintain contact with your employer and fellow employees if you think you might want your job back when your kids are older. Send holiday cards, call just to chat, and go out to lunch with former colleagues occasionally.

If you loved your job, tell your boss! Be completely honest, that you never thought you'd want to be a stay-at-home mom, but now you do. Your honesty should be evident, and your boss should respect you for that. When the responsibilities at home lighten up and you want to return to the workforce, you'll be glad your relationship with your former employer is still on good terms.

Feeling guilty when you let someone down makes sense, but it doesn't help either you or your employer. It's perfectly fine to apologize for not knowing in advance how you would feel after being home with your baby. You can even apologize for not coming back to work if that makes you feel better. But I assure you, this happens all the time in the work world, and while employers aren't happy about it, they aren't surprised either. Just tell your employer promptly and professionally, and be glad that you are able to make the choice that works best for you.

I worked outside of the home when my first child was little, but now that there are two, I plan to stay home. Will my first child be upset that I stayed home for her sister, but not for her?

Unless you feel particularly guilty about your choice to stay home now, I would be very surprised if your first child gets upset. In fact, if you manage this well, choosing to stay at home now should be a positive experience for you all. Explain to your kids in language appropriate to their ages why you are planning to stay at home. If you are comfortable with the change in plans, everybody should be able to understand and accept the wisdom of your decision, and no feelings will be hurt.

Isabel worked full time while her children were very young. She had excellent child care and a job she'd worked hard to get. As her two daughters got older, though, she felt she wanted to be at home with them. Her husband was by then earning a bit more money, and her child-care provider wanted to retire. She decided to stay home with them when they entered middle school, feeling that this was when she was needed at home most. Her daughters were delighted that she was home when they'd get home from school every day, and never questioned why she was around so much more for the two of them than for just the first.

If the older one questions you or expresses sadness that you were not as available to her when she was little as you now are to her sibling, listen carefully and reassure her that you have always loved her very much. Explain that one of the reasons for choosing to stay home now is that you want to be able to spend more time with her. Show her that you plan to use this opportunity to spend time with each child. Your loving and attentive interactions with your children will alleviate any anxiety on their parts, and guilt on yours.

If you are matter-of-fact about your change of heart and working status, your kids will be accepting, too. Explain how circumstances are different now, that your decision about staying home is based on the needs of the *whole* family; they will not assume that you love one more than the other. Be very clear that it is your desires, or the family needs, finances, job, or baby-sitter situation that has changed, and that you are thrilled to be able to make this switch for them and for yourself.

I love staying at home with my kids, but I wonder—having given up my career for the time being, am I a terrible role model for my kids?

What kind of role model do you want to be for your kids? In my mind, there are many ways to be an admirable role model, and whether you work outside the home or not is not the most important factor. Think about what you want to teach your kids about yourself, about love and marriage, about work, respect, and making choices.

- Are you happy and fulfilled being a stay-at-home mom?
- Do you have interests and a life beyond your role as mother?
- Is your marriage loving, mutually respectful, and satisfying?
- Is it clear that you don't resent or regret staying at home?
- Do you feel respected by your kids?
- Do your children know that you are staying at home by choice?

The best role model I can imagine is a mother who is kind, loving, and comfortable with her decisions and her life. If you are staying at home because your husband demands that you do, or if you hate being at home and desperately miss work, if you feel that women should be working outside the home, your discontent will become evident to them. Then, no matter how hard you try, being a stay-at-home mom will make you appear to be a martyr, and you will be the bad role model you fear you are.

On the other hand, if you are home by choice, if you value the time spent with your kids, if your husband and children respect all that you do for them, and if you are generally content, then you are showing your kids that it is good to do what seems right to you. Nurturing your family by choice, without losing yourself, is a great gift and provides an excellent role model.

I think I'm a great mom, but I feel so inefficient. How can I get more done?

Being efficient while raising kids is a challenge; moms nationwide struggle to prepare nutritious meals, keep up with housework, help with homework, and still try to have some fun. Many stay-at-home moms find that they must develop shortcuts and tricks. Rather than offer you specific ideas to streamline your days, let me pass along the more general suggestions that have worked for countless moms trying to wade through their days.

- ❧ Clarify your priorities. Figure out what's really important to the well-being of your family and don't waste time on things that don't matter.
- ❧ Lower your standards. For example, do not vacuum everyday unless you have pets that shed excessively or a health reason to do so.
- ❧ Make lists to help you keep track of what needs to be done or purchased.
- ❧ Keep a calendar or date book in a conspicuous place on which you write all of your appointments, dates, due dates for kids' school assignments, and so on.
- ❧ Simplify your life. Don't offer to do something when you feel overwhelmed.
- ❧ Share tasks. Use carpools, co-chair a committee, and enlist your kids' and husband's support rather than take on all responsibilities by yourself.

- Expect your children to do age-appropriate chores as soon as they are able. Even the littlest kids can put toys in a bin when they are done. Increase your expectations of your children's contributions to household tasks in keeping with their increasing abilities.

- Plan your tasks wisely. Divide jobs up so that they can be done in small time frames, and use downtime effectively. For example, you can make a marinade for the chicken breasts in a matter of minutes while the kids are busy playing a game. You can balance your checkbook while waiting for your child at the dentist.

- Work on tasks that take longer or will suffer if interrupted when your children are otherwise occupied. Once you can count on an extended nap time, or you know your kids will be at school or a friend's house for a couple of hours, you can use that time to do the jobs that need your sustained attention.

- Teach your children to be patient when you are busy with something that needs to be finished so that interruptions are minimal and only when necessary. If your children are very little, have special toys for them to play with while you finish up a project, or talk to them about what you are doing to soothe them while they wait for your full attention.

- Hire help if you can afford it, whether to baby-sit or to clean your home occasionally.

- Maintain a sense of humor.

- Be willing to live in the moment. Your children are young and at home with you for a relatively short period of your life. Enjoy each other; the way you relate to your children and husband is vastly more important than your efficiency or lack thereof.

Most stay-at-home moms find the demands of motherhood surprisingly overwhelming, and they expect that they should do the bulk of the housework even if they never did it before they had kids, or if they have no talent for cooking, organizing, or cleaning. And it's hard to figure out sometimes whether you should be playing with the kids or folding laundry. Try to remind yourself that it's okay to be less than the perfect homemaker. Give yourself some time to figure out how to get things done, take shortcuts when you can, and remember that enjoying each other's company is a major priority.

I chose to be an at-home mom and I'm glad I did, so then why do I feel so unimportant?

The stay-at-home mother is focused on helping others achieve and grow. When you do a good job, your family thrives; your kids develop into healthy, contributing members of society, your husband feels supported in his efforts to provide financially for the family, and you appear to do it all effortlessly. Although your contributions to your family are enormous, they are often invisible to others and include some very tedious and thankless chores. It isn't that you don't matter tremendously; it's just that a lot of the most important things you do (like being there to listen, kiss a scraped knee, take a forgotten lunch to school, or run to the drug store for glue sticks and poster board), you do so graciously and seamlessly that they often go unnoticed.

No wonder you feel unimportant. Of course, when the soccer jersey isn't washed or dinner is not so tasty, your husband or kids will notice; your best efforts, though, even in the most grateful family, sometimes seem taken for granted. One of the most difficult facts of stay-at-home motherhood is that too often, mothers feel unimportant and undervalued. And one of the trickiest parts of being a good mother is to be able to take excellent care of your family without being taken advantage of or feeling like a martyr.

You need to feel good enough about your mothering that you aren't so reliant on praise from others to feel important. Make a list of all you do in a week to make your family's life more comfortable. If necessary, carry a notepad with you at all times and write down each task you do for others in the home. By the end of a week, you'll have a better idea of how much work you do for your family's needs. If you undervalue your own role in the family, read your list whenever you feel unimportant. Seeing all that you do in black and white should help you recognize how vital you are.

You may also want to reeducate your family about what it is you do all day to make their lives more comfortable. If your family treats you as if you don't much matter, it's time for a family meeting. Show your husband and kids your list so that they can see just how much of your day is devoted to keeping your family comfortable. Your intention here should not be to make *them* feel guilty for all that you do, but to help them see that in your family, everyone's efforts are important. Just because you don't get graded or receive a paycheck doesn't mean that your contributions to the family aren't worthy of respect.

Talk to your family when you are feeling unimportant. Tell them that while you love being a stay-at-home mom, you also need to be appreciated for what you do. Make sure that you and your family members say "please" and "thank you" to each other, including to you, whenever someone does something to help another, even regular household chores. Show your children and husband genuine appreciation for what they offer the family, be proud of your contributions to your family, and you will start to feel appreciated in return.

I know being an at-home mom is right for me, so then why do I feel so uninteresting?

You feel uninteresting partly because your interests have become narrower than they were before you became a stay-at-home mom, and partly because people frequently assume that moms have no interests outside their families. Being home with kids is very different than working outside the home. The challenges you face tend to be personal, and the increments of change as you watch your children grow up and your family develop are miniscule and hard to measure. The work of a stay-at-home mom is insulated from the rest of the world and filled with repetitive tasks and details that no one outside your family circle will care about nearly as much as you. While that's plenty to keep you busy and entertained, your enthusiasm about little Alan finally turning over by himself is hard to share.

You are not uninteresting; your focus has just shifted. As soon as you have a bit more free time, you may actually find that your stay-at-home status allows you to develop hobbies and skills that working full time did not. While your kids are in school or at dance class, you may be able to read the newspaper or novels, take up oil painting or belly dancing, and become a more well-rounded person than ever before. Take a class, read about some subject you never had time to before, take walks, or do volunteer work. Most stay-at-home moms learn to fit the pursuit of their own interests into children's schedules and ultimately become more interesting than ever.

What makes a person interesting is not what they do all day, but the person they are and their thoughts and feelings about the world. You don't have to be boring just because you take care of your family, and in reality, you probably aren't. Even if you choose not to pursue new interests, your love and concern for your family, your observations of their development, and your willingness to take care of other people can be fascinating.

I'm glad I'm a stay-at-home mom, but how can I deal with feeling bored much of the time?

Not everyone finds staying home with their kids to be the most scintillating thing they've ever done. Many stay-at-home moms agree that the day-to-day, repetitive nature of caring for a home and young children can be tedious at times. But then, many women who work outside the home are bored, too, and lots of stay-at-home moms don't remember how frequently they were bored or dissatisfied while they were working.

Although you are glad to have the opportunity to be a stay-at-home mom, you may not yet have found the way to make it work well for you. It will be in your best interest, and ultimately your family's best interest, to find ways to remain excited and entertained while being a stay-at-home mom.

- Do you miss adult conversation? Make time each day to call or email a friend, plan an outing with a friend at least once a week, or join a class.
- Do you miss your old job? Call former coworkers and meet for lunch. Join or create a reading group in your area of interest. Help one morning a week in your children's school,

or organize a block party. Find out if you can work a little bit from home or do some volunteering until you are ready to return to the workforce.

- ❧ If your children are all in school, you have many hours a day when you are not actively engaged in child care. Follow an old hobby or take up something new. Reorganize your closets or write a novel. You now have time and energy to expend on your own interests, at least for a few hours every day. Take advantage of this!

- ❧ If your kids are still home, you might need to find new things to do together. Go on field trips, visit friends, or put on a puppet show. Take trips to the library, zoo, or even a shopping mall. Take the kids and everyone out of the house!

- ❧ Find ways to be active in your church, synagogue, or community. Many towns have organizations that serve common interests, and many offer lectures as well as opportunities to help others.

Sometimes women who stay at home become so isolated and narrowly focused that they feel a bit bored and lonely. They lose sight of the possibilities for connecting with others in meaningful ways or feel that their own interests "should" be set aside while the kids are young. But moms need to be fulfilled by more than even excellent mothering. Search your local newspaper, call your town's chamber of commerce, and check out park district and YMCA offerings, and you'll likely find something to keep you interested.

I feel guilty that I love it when my kids are all in school and I have the house to myself and I dread summer and school holidays. Am I too selfish?

Well, if you are too selfish, you are in very good company. Personally, I think that enjoying the time your kids are at school (or at camp or friends' houses) is normal, and most stay-at-home moms I know are in total agreement. As much as moms love their kids, having a few hours a day alone in your home is very nice. You can get a lot done or you can relax and do nothing, and you have no little ones tugging on you asking you to play or feed them. You can go to the bathroom alone or even take a nap and know your children are safe and entertained. Why wouldn't you appreciate that time?

Being a stay-at-home mom doesn't require you to give up all your previous interests and needs (although it sometimes seems that way). Of course, you are dedicated to caring for your children, but you are also a whole person. Taking care of young children can be exhausting and demanding: you don't get predictable or consistent breaks, and you have little time to yourself. Most women need some time to unwind, time to get things done around the house without interruption, and time to be a complete person, not only a mom. When school is in session, those breaks are provided; when school is out, you are back in charge of your kids for what often feels like a very long day.

Lots of moms resent school vacations and those odd school days off for teacher conferences or holidays. The rhythm of your week is disrupted and the children, although often excited to have the day off, need to be entertained. There are more meals to prepare and clean up after, and instead of having that time that you've come to count on to yourself, you become the social director for the day.

There are lots of ways to handle this.

- Plan ahead. Most schools provide calendars including all days off. Make sure you plan your own projects, appointments, and so on to accommodate the school calendar so that you don't need to scramble for child care at the last minute and you can still get your hair cut.
- Don't even try to follow your usual child-free routine if your children are still young. If you expect to work out, go shopping, talk to your friends—whatever adult projects you usually tackle when the kids are at school—you'll be disappointed. Make child-centered plans instead or arrange for child care.
- Many moms use those days to take care of details for their kids. Dental appointments are great to schedule for school holidays that aren't also national holidays. Make the appointment as far in advance as possible, as other moms have figured this out, too. Getting check-ups or other chores done on school holidays works well because it gives your kids something to do, and you don't have to go rushing around in the late afternoons doing everything necessary between school and bedtime.
- Plan for fun trips for days off, inviting another compatible family along if possible. It's great to go to that museum you've always wanted to visit on days off from school.
- Make play dates for your kids for those days.
- View the school days off as a special time for you with your kids. Forget about your usual chores and hang out with your kids. Go for a picnic, visit a park, or take a long walk. Make the day special so that you enjoy it, too.
- Arrange with a friend to swap who takes the kids when school is out. That way you'd still have some of those days to yourself, and so would your friend.

◈ Make the day different; stay in your pajamas all day, eat special foods (all one color, or dinner foods for breakfast, pancakes for dinner), or make paper chains with which to festoon the dining room. You don't need to spend much money or be all that creative to enjoy being with your kids instead of finding them a burden.

You are not a bad person because you don't like it when your schedule is thrown off by school not being in session. Even pre-school offers moms at least six child-free hours a week, and those hours are precious. Don't worry that you're a bad mom; you're just being honest. Accept that the kids are going to be around a lot more than you expected and try to make the time more appealing and an opportunity for all of you.

How can I learn to tolerate being so isolated?

Things used to be different. Only a couple of generations ago, when women didn't have so many socially acceptable choices, newlyweds tended to live pretty close to their parents' homes and they had their children at more or less the same age as their best friends and siblings. Women could be stay-at-home moms without feeling isolated because there was always someone nearby to share a cup of coffee or a chat. Nowadays, though, women have children at any age from teens to their forties, go away to college, develop careers, and live in communities miles and miles from relatives or old friends. When they stay home with their children, they might not really know any of their neighbors or have family or friends close enough to visit. Stay-at-home motherhood can then feel very isolating.

If you are not a person who enjoys solitude, being a stay-at-home mom can be very lonely. Fortunately, there are many ways to combat that:

- Lauren, mother of two-year-old Matt, goes to the grocery store nearly every day. She says that having a daily outing with guaranteed adult contact keeps her sane, and her husband loves the fresh meals she is able to prepare.
- Anita joined a gym with baby-sitting. She loves getting a regular workout; her two-year-old calls the baby-sitting room "school" and loves it, and Anita has made some good friends there.
- Many communities have classes for mothers and/or young children. Sometimes signing a child up for swim class not only teaches the child to swim, it also offers Mom some much needed time with other moms.
- Going for walks or on field trips with your children also decreases a mom's sense of isolation. Being out in public and having casual conversations with other adults eases the loneliness.
- Make play dates with other children and invite the parents along, even when your children are old enough to play on their own. You'll get to know the other mothers and have some companionship.
- Be a little bold. If you see another mother with her kids when on a walk in the park, or in a coffee house, stop and say hello. Admire her children, talk about the weather, but somehow strike up a conversation. If you seem compatible, suggest you meet there the next week. Yes, this can feel very awkward, but I know several women, including myself, who made great and lasting friendships

from moms they met at museums, parks, and grocery stores.

- ❧ Start your own playgroup. Ask your church or synagogue administrator, your pediatrician or obstetrician, to allow you to put up a notice in his or her office, or to pass your name along to other stay-at-home moms who might be interested.
- ❧ The Internet has provided support to many a mom. Check out the infinite possibilities of websites geared to moms, join a chat room, or start your own.

Although spending the bulk of your day at home with your kids can feel very lonely, seeking out other mothers will help. It's pretty safe to assume that if you are feeling isolated, that nice-looking mom on the next block, or the one you used to talk with in your childbirth preparation class, may feel lonely, too.

I miss the positive feedback I used to get from working. How can I handle being a stay-at-home mom when I miss those verbal pats on the back so much?

In the working world, if you do your work, you see results in a sale, a product made, a project completed; there are verbal and financial rewards. At home, the work seems repetitious and endless, you get no paycheck, and rarely does someone commend you on dusting particularly well that day. Lots of stay-at-home moms miss getting that clearly defined positive reinforcement for what they do. Those mothers need to teach their families to show appreciation when appropriate, and they need to learn to get gratification from a job well done, whether or not anyone else notices.

"Please" and "thank you" go a long way in helping a mom feel appreciated. As soon as your children are born, teach them to request help from you with a "please" and to thank you when you have done something for them. The best way I've found for teaching kids to respond politely and to offer praise generously is to be polite and verbally generous yourself. Make sure that when you ask your child to pick up his toys, you include a "please," and when the toys are put away, thank him for doing such a good job.

Treat your husband respectfully, too, thanking him whenever he does the dishes, even if that's his normal job. Tell your husband how much it means to you when he thanks you for taking his suit to the dry cleaners, or for making his favorite meal, regardless of whether it's expected of you or not. Expressing appreciation openly and often becomes routine, hearing it feels good, and you will all benefit from those verbal gifts.

Although stay-at-home moms do a lot of scut work and often miss many of the social, economic, and ego-gratifying benefits of employment, being able to be a stay-at-home mom is a luxury of which many moms who work outside the home can only dream. Sometimes, when you are feeling especially taken for granted, the perks of staying at home get forgotten. When you are feeling particularly under-appreciated, remind yourself that you get to decide on a whim to drop everything and go for a walk on a beautiful day, you are actively and intimately involved in the details of your children's lives, and you are in many ways your own boss. Self-employed people must learn to acknowledge themselves and their own achievements; knowing in your heart that you are an outstanding mother may sometimes need to suffice for you.

Words of praise from others are only one way of knowing that you are valued. Seeing your family happy and healthy is another.

Treat each other well and accept that those pats on the back you need can come in many forms and from many sources, including from within.

I work all day long, caring for the kids, my husband, and our home, yet I can't see the benefits of all my efforts. When will I know if all this devotion will pay off?

Well, that depends on what kind of pay off you are looking for. If you are hoping for some shining moment when it becomes clear that because of your contributions to your family they have all achieved every personal, social, and professional goal they or you have ever imagined, you may have a very long wait. If you're seeking public adulation or some objective event to tell you it was all worthwhile, that's not likely to happen soon, either. Family life just doesn't work that way.

Alternatively, if you want to know when you will be certain that being a stay-at-home mom was right for you and your family, that could be now. You made the choice that seems right for you. There are no guarantees that being a stay-at-home mom will create superior, more contented children or anything measurable at all, but what you do for your family pays off daily. You work hard, love your children and your husband, and try to do and be what they need without losing yourself in the process. When you see your family grow, watch your children enjoy themselves and each other, that's the payoff. If you are a stay-at-home mom looking for more than that, you might want to look elsewhere.

If you resent being at home, if your devotion feels more like a pointless sacrifice, then this isn't the right situation for you. The payoff you seek may never come, and if you feel continually disappointed or dissatisfied with your own labors, you would be doing everyone a favor by finding a .child-care provider who wants to be there. Although it can be difficult to remain faithful that what you do as a mother has value when you don't often see tangible results for all your efforts, in order to be content as a stay-at-home mom, you must ultimately maintain that faith.

The details of what you do or don't do for yourself or for your family don't matter so much. Children and families need different things at different times; being a stay-at-home mom may benefit one child more than another. The best of mothers occasionally mess up, and the worst mothers often have children who do okay. If you are a stay-at-home mom because that seems right to you and your family, then it probably is right. Relax and seek confirmation that your devotion is worth it in the daily interactions with your loved ones.

I'm busy with the house, kids, and errands from the moment I get up until I go to bed, yet there is nothing to show for it. How can I prove that I'm not just sitting on my duff all day?

Anybody who has ever been a stay-at home mom, or even a part-time stay-at-home mom, knows how hard you work. We also know that much of what you do cannot be measured or seen. Consider the most important things you do as a mother, and you will feel better about proving what you do all day.

❦ You listen to your kids. You pay attention to their concerns, their interests, their joys, and their fears. You make it very clear that they matter.

- You help them. You take them to school, arrange their social lives, prepare meals, pack lunches, help them with their homework, and do their laundry.
- You have fun with them. You teach them to sing your favorite songs; you dance, and play with them.
- You have a high regard for them. When they say, "Mommy, watch this!" you are there watching and admiring.
- You provide structure. When they are tired, you sometimes notice it before they do. If they want to play with friends when they have music lessons, you help them figure out how to do all that they want and need to do. You help them understand the consequences of their actions.
- You provide love. You show them that you love them, even though they are not perfect. They see the pleasure you take in their existence. They feel lovable because of your unconditional love.
- You encourage and supervise play dates.
- You encourage their interests and support their activities.
- In addition to taking care of their emotional, social, and educational needs, you also make sure there's enough to eat, clean clothes, and a clean and reasonably tidy house.

Yes, you do work hard, and it's true that there is little that you have to show for it. But even though your efforts seem invisible and intangible, your input is invaluable. Don't worry about proving what a hard worker you are. The immeasurable jobs of motherhood are what ultimately count far more than how many diapers you may have changed.

Ever since I've become a stay-at-home mom, I don't know who or what I am anymore. What happened, and how do I get *me* back?

Natasha, the stay-at-home mother of three, loved being a mom, but she also felt that motherhood kind of blotted out all the other roles she played. Because she dedicated herself to mothering her children, at least while they were still little, she lost touch with friends from her previous life and work. She rarely hired sitters because she wasn't bringing in any income, so she also stopped some of her favorite pastimes. She no longer played tennis or met her friends for coffee.

Some women find it difficult to integrate motherhood into their lives, especially if they feel that they *should* focus entirely on the children. But children thrive when they have mothers who are also whole people with ideas, tastes, and passions of their own. Your being a real and complete person helps them become real themselves, so it isn't even selfish to maintain your identity while you are a stay-at-home mom.

Under most normal circumstances, your children will eventually become independent, grow up, and leave home. If you're totally devoted to your kids and only to them, if you feel you've lost yourself in the process, you do yourself, your marriage, and possibly the kids themselves no favors in the long run. You provide your children with a role model unaware of herself and unable to recognize or fulfill her own needs, you damage your marriage by putting it on the back burner, and you inflate your children's sense of their place in the world. When it's time for your children to move out, you may be left feeling empty and without purpose, with little connection to your spouse, and the children may feel guilty about leaving you or inappropriately responsible for your continued happiness.

Mothers need and deserve to be whole people, and it's good for your marriage and your kids for you to fulfill your own needs, too. You don't have to care for your loved ones to the exclusion of attending to your own dreams; you can be a tremendously attentive and loving mother while still pursuing your own interests. For example, if you enjoyed art before you became a mother, you don't have to move to an art studio and paint all day long, but you can allow yourself several hours a week of working on projects that make you feel yourself again.

You can find yourself by remembering what gave you pleasure and what excited you before motherhood eclipsed those other parts of yourself. Nurture yourself. Devote time each week to your own personal passions. Revisit old hobbies, reconnect with old friends, and reclaim your interests and personality. Taking care of yourself and your marriage as well as you take care of your children is one of the best things you can do for your entire family.

Having chosen to be a stay-at-home mom, I'm with my kids all the time. So why do I feel guilty when I go out with my friends, leaving them with a sitter?

Too many stay-at-home moms believe that if they've chosen not to work outside the home, they should be totally devoted to taking care of the kids. They feel uncomfortable or guilty when they leave the children to visit with pals, run errands the children would find unbearable, or even to do volunteer work. Most of the time, this guilt comes from the overwhelming and unrealistic idea that a stay-at-home mom should be constantly available to her children.

Some women feel guilty that, having chosen to be stay-at-home moms, they don't want to spend every waking moment of every day with their children. They worry that if they long for adult companionship or wish for a couple of hours to pursue their adult interests, they are somehow not adequately devoted mothers. Some also fret that because they do not work for pay, they do not deserve to have a break, especially when taking that break entails paying for a sitter.

While feeling bad that you do occasionally want or need to get away from your children may be pretty common, needing adult contact or time alone also makes sense. As long as the children are well cared for and you can afford to pay for the sitter, then I see no problem here. What you want is reasonable, manageable financially, and actually helps you be a more satisfied person. That all sounds good.

The value of a mother is not measured in hours spent with her children, but in the interactions themselves. If the time you spend with your children is enjoyable, if you listen to your kids, support them, and guide them lovingly, then time away from them, even with a sitter, will do no harm. If you can afford it, it will probably even be good for you all, as you will be less likely to resent your stay-at-home status when you have some freedom to pursue other interests, to be yourself as well as your children's mom.

I love being home, but what can I do about feeling so guilty that I'm not contributing to the family income?

If you love being at home and your family is able to manage financially, there's no need to feel guilty. You may need to figure out what you are truly feeling, though, because if everything is great, you shouldn't be feeling so bad. Honing in on what's making you so uncomfortable about this arrangement should help alleviate any guilt or allow you to correct an imbalance if there is one.

Did you decide that you wanted to be a stay-at-home mom without checking with your husband about how he feels? If you and your husband did not come to an agreement about how you were going to manage your family's needs, you may need to make sure that your husband isn't overwhelmed or resentful that you're enjoying being at home while he's slaving away at work. Your guilt may be a result of feeling like you somehow pulled something over on your husband. Share your concerns with your mate; if he's unhappy that he's the sole breadwinner, maybe you can find a way to do something to ease the burden on him. If he's content, though, you'll be able to relax and fully enjoy your stay-at-home status.

Has money become too tight? If your husband's salary no longer stretches far enough to cover all your expenses, or if you haven't curtailed your spending to match your income, your staying at home may be a problem, and that's why you're feeling bad. You may need to reassess your budget, cut back on your expenditures, find less expensive housing, or somehow supplement his income. If you can't keep up with the bills on Dad's paychecks alone, no wonder you're feeling a bit guilty.

Do you feel that you should be earning money or that you should be working? Thanks to all the choices now available to women, moms who choose to stay at home often feel that they should be contributing financially to the family even if there is no actual financial need. If this describes your emotions, then getting a part-time job might make you feel a bit better.

The positive side of having lots of choices is that whatever choice you make, there are many women who will be supportive of you. If you and your husband agree that you can manage comfortably without your bringing in a paycheck, then don't beat yourself up over what society says you should or shouldn't do. Enjoy your opportunity to be a stay-at-home mom guilt-free.

I chose to be a stay-at-home mom, but I sometimes feel jealous that my husband gets to go to work every day. Does this make sense?

Of course it makes sense, and there are a lot of stay-at-home moms who share your jealousy. Just because you chose to stay at home doesn't mean that you'll love every minute, or that you won't miss certain aspects of your former life. Watching your husband go off to work every day stirs up memories of dressing nicely for work, having daily contact with other adults, receiving a paycheck, and other perks of the working life. Although staying home may be mostly wonderful, sometimes the lure of returning to your previous, more independent and professional self turns you green.

Megan, mother of four-year-old Charlie and seven-year-old Nick, admits envying her husband's commute to and from work, alone in the car, no one else's radio tastes to consider, no squabbling to monitor, no juice boxes spilling. Natalie, a former economist, felt those stabs of jealousy whenever her husband walked out the door dressed in a clean suit, knowing that he'd be spending the day with grown-ups, being congratulated whenever he does a particularly good job, and nobody spitting up on his shoulder.

Periodically feeling jealous of your husband may represent some ambivalence about having decided to be a stay-at-home mom. Ambivalence is normal, though; no mom experiences either staying at home or working outside the home as uniformly blissful. Unless your ambivalence is overwhelming, don't worry about it. If you are mostly contented with being a stay-at-home mom, then intermittently resenting your husband's going off to work, particularly if you enjoyed working in your pre-mommy years, can be expected. Share your feelings with your husband; he may be feeling jealous of you, too, and that communication may help you remain close and appreciate how devoted each of you is to your family.

If your jealousy consumes you, though, you may have a bigger problem. Your marriage may be off balance, or you may not be as suited to staying at home full time as you'd hoped. Use that jealousy to help you connect to the core problem. You may need to be working outside the home simply for your own mental health, or it may be that working will help you to maintain a more equal footing in your marriage. Either way, if your marriage needs help or you just miss working more than you realized, you deserve to feel better. While occasionally feeling wistful about the workplace is normal, feeling uncomfortably and constantly jealous of your husband is not. When it's more than just a twinge, jealousy hurts. Talk it over with your husband and seek counseling if you need help sorting this all out.

As a stay-at-home mom, shouldn't I be a great cook and housekeeper?

Being a terrible housekeeper does not make you a terrible wife or mother, but it's understandable that you feel bad about it. The bulk of the cooking and cleaning typically becomes the stay-at-home parent's responsibility, regardless of interest or talents. You do need to have a home that is clean and tidy enough to be safe, and food available that is edible and healthful, but you can still be a fantastic wife and mother even if your house is a mess and your cooking makes everyone gag. You may need help in both areas, but please don't confuse excellent mothering or wifehood with excellence with a broom or spatula.

As long as no one is threatening to call the health department, and you can see much of the floor in most rooms, chances are that your cleaning and tidying, while not impressive, are probably also not dangerous or unhealthy. If the mess in your home truly keeps getting away from you, seek assistance. The easiest, though most expensive, solution to this problem is to hire someone to come in on a regular basis and do whatever jobs you do not do. If you can afford it, hiring help to clean and tidy up your home can save a great deal of emotional turmoil. Your home will be clean and sparkling, and by hiring someone who does this professionally, it will be done quickly and well.

If you can't hire someone, or if you cling to the idea that a mother who takes care of the house well provides a better role model (as a sloppy mom, I don't fully agree), find a friend who'll teach you how to take care of your home. Make a list of housekeeping tasks that must get done, set aside a day every week, or two hours a few times a week, during which you will not answer the phone, watch TV, or take a nap until you have done the cleaning on that list. Put forth a concerted effort, enlist friends to help, give your children jobs that they can manage, and just bite the bullet and do it. And accept that a person who isn't naturally inclined to keeping a tidy house may never be able to rival the sitcom home she sees on TV, except maybe for *Roseanne* reruns.

Providing excellent meals does not have to involve cooking. Take advantage of the many already prepared entrée and side dish items available in most supermarkets. Bring food in from restaurants on occasion. Ask each of your friends to teach you how to make one easy but edible meal, and then repeat as often as tolerable. If your husband can cook, have him make large quantities of freezable dishes for future consumption.

If you have a skill you can barter, do so. Baby-sit your friends' children while they cook or clean for you. Take care of a friend's garden while she bakes lasagna, or sew Halloween costumes in exchange for a day of laundry. While you may not excel at the domestic arts, you may still be a spectacular wife, mother, and friend. Be grateful for what you are good at, and get support to do the rest.

I'm embarrassed to admit it, but I watch way too much television. If it helps me stay sane, should I still feel so guilty about it?

I think television has gotten a bad reputation. Many stay-at-home moms swear that they will never use the TV as a baby-sitter or become hooked on the daytime soaps or talk shows. Once they find themselves home with a baby or young children all day, day after day, many normal women will occasionally become desperate to hear another adult voice. Lots of respectable women use the television or radio to help them get through the day, despite their earlier intentions not to succumb.

Unless you park your children in front of the TV every day for hours on end, or you yourself get so caught up in your daytime lineup of "entertainment" that you ignore your children's needs, television watching shouldn't cause you shame. Use it judiciously, sparingly, and appropriately. If you are really worried that TV has taken over your life, start keeping track of how much television you actually watch each day. If you turn on the high quality child-oriented shows for your toddler while you fold the laundry, that's probably just fine. If you limit your favorite daytime shows to when the baby naps, that's okay, too.

In general, I think TV has saved a lot of stay-at-home moms' minds. I think in reasonable doses, especially when you watch programs with your child, television can even be good. Several public television shows have been credited with teaching children their letters and numbers, as well as presenting some very positive social concepts. Watch children's shows with your kids. Explain anything that seems confusing, including things that indicate moral or value judgments. Keep in mind their level of intellectual and emotional development.

Do not allow your kids to watch shows that present material you believe to be beyond your children's emotional or intellectual understanding or that you find offensive. If your favorite show is a soap opera with lots of steamy sex scenes, tape it so that you can watch during your kids' nap time. If your worry is that you watch too much TV, make sure that you and your children have an active social life and get out of the house at least several days a week. Then watching the tube a bit every day will be just fine.

Of course, television can be harmful if it becomes a substitute for interpersonal interaction or physical activity. If you find yourself in front of the television all day, if you turn down play dates or refuse to schedule outings during your favorite shows, or if you have no other ideas for keeping your children occupied, then you might want to rethink how you spend your days. If you can't relate to your children and use TV as a substitute for more direct interaction, then you need some help. If your TV viewing is an indication of a more serious problem, get help, because you and your kids will feel better when your relationships are broader.

On the other hand, for most stay-at-home moms, watching TV is something they do in limited amounts, and within appropriate limits, it may not be exactly laudable, but it is certainly okay.

I feel guilty that I get to stay home with our children while my husband has to work. Is that normal?

It's kind of sweet, but guilt isn't very productive. You are lucky that you feel so good about being able to stay at home, and your husband is lucky that you appreciate his working so hard. So why do you feel guilty? Understand that you and your husband have chosen together to divide the many aspects of helping a family grow. You appreciate the opportunity to be at home with your kids, while your husband should also appreciate his ability to go to work without having to worry about who's taking care of the kids and house. That seems well balanced to me.

Maybe instead of feeling guilty, you and your husband should show how much you appreciate each other more often. After all, knowing you are at home with the kids gives your husband the peace of mind to focus completely on his work. His financial support allows you to focus completely on raising your family. While the division of labor may not always seem equal, if it works for your family and you all feel comfortable with the arrangement, then it is equitable and fair, and that's lovely.

Ideally, both husband and wife should feel comfortable with the balance between working and staying home that you've chosen. You may not be content 100 percent of the time, but if you generally are pleased that you are able to stay at home, your husband accepts that he will be the working parent, and you can manage on one income, then settle down and enjoy your freedom to choose. You both win with any arrangement that fills everybody's needs without undue burden or pressure on anyone. Unless your husband wants to be a stay-at-home dad, you have struck a workable balance, and no one needs to feel anything but good.

Endnote

When we are little, we think our parents know everything. We believe that they really have answers to all our questions, that a kiss can heal a scraped elbow, that no one is as beautiful or smart as our mother, as funny and wise as our father. Kids with generally good, well-meaning, thoughtful, and loving parents never consider that those parents worry about how to parent them, struggle with decisions about how much they work, whether or not to punish, when to say "yes" or when to say "no." When we are little, we believe that our parents simply know how to be parents, that they don't give parenthood a lot of thought, and that what they do is usually okay.

As we get older, we venture out into other people's homes, we spend time with others, we learn about the world firsthand, and we begin to see that not all families are alike. We begin to observe how other children live and how other parents set rules, love and guide their children, spend their money and time, and give gifts. We see that some families do lots of interesting things together, others travel, some work round the clock. Some kids seem free and easy with their parents; some seem constantly on the alert, intensely respectful, maybe fearful. Some parents seem to dote on their children's accomplishments, some push their kids always to do more and better, some value good grades, others value athleticism, and some pay their kids very little attention at all. We think about what kind of parents we wish we had, and then we wonder what kind of parents we'll be.

I think that people enter parenthood with an abundance of ideas and hopes. If they are thoughtful about their parenting, and I believe that the vast majority of parents really, truly want to be good parents, they think about what they can do or not do to be the best parents they can be. They want to be everything their parents were, or perhaps, everything their parents were not. They think about good and bad memories of their own childhoods, they watch friends and relatives becoming parents, and they model themselves on what they see and admire. They read books, listen to experts on talk shows, and consider what it means to be a good parent. They do their best to be good parents, to do the right thing, and they feel bad when they believe that they have let themselves or their children down.

We pay very little attention to how what is going on in our own lives may impact how we are as parents. We don't tend to consider what our own level of maturity is, what our own emotional issues are, or even that these kinds of things may have a profound impact on how we are as parents. I believe that parents are people, too, and that people continue to grow emotionally their entire lives. As a psychotherapist, I've worked with troubled people for many years, people who are parents themselves, or the parents of troubled kids, as well as many, many grownups who trace the beginnings of their emotional or relationship problems to some pretty distressing associations or interactions with their own parents while they were growing up. Still, I have yet to find one parent who didn't want to be a good parent, who didn't believe that he or she had tried really hard to be a good parent. Almost without exception, parents really want to do right by their kids.

But even the most well-intentioned, well-informed, well-educated people sometimes mess up. My experience has shown me that people continue to learn and understand the world and themselves differently as they age. While they want to be great parents, they also want to get satisfaction from the world. They want love and friendship and meaningful experiences. They want to get ahead in their careers, they want gratifying relationships with peers, they want to pursue a satisfying hobby, or they just want to sit by the fire and read a good book without interruption. I don't believe that adulthood is a static life stage, or that anyone can be totally self-sacrificing or void of self-interest. Nor do I believe that people who are parents should. But figuring out when to meet your own needs, when it's okay to be selfish and when it isn't, and even being clear enough about who you are as a person, let alone as a parent, directly relates to your behavior as a parent, and good parenting can be very complicated to achieve.

When you want to be a great parent, yet you find yourself getting in your own way, you feel pretty bad. Mostly, we identify this feeling as guilt. I hope this book will help mothers take the time to think about what they do and feel as parents. I hope that knowing that most mothers feel guilty often unnecessarily will help ease some of that guilt, and I hope that reading this book will help moms understand that often what they do as a mother is absolutely fine.

I also hope that reading this book will help mothers learn when their instincts are good to follow and when they should take a few deep breaths and think before they act. Perhaps most importantly, especially for those mothers who feel responsible for the mental health and happiness of their kids, I hope that readers will learn that it's okay not to be perfect. In fact, imperfection is both inevitable and desirable. Kids do well when they know that their mothers love, respect, and listen to them. Kids appreciate honesty and thoughtfulness much more than exquisitely presented meals or up-to-the-minute furnishings. Kids want to be loved for the real people that they are, and they will love their parents, quirks and all, when they feel that love.

I hope this book helps readers to accept themselves and their children and be tolerant of all their loved ones, including themselves. Remember, it's okay to feel a little guilty when you do something you know you shouldn't; just apologize and try not to mess up the next time. It's also appropriate to feel bad when your children are hurting, or when a conflict causes disappointment, regardless of whether or not you personally caused that pain. But it's pointless to drown in guilt over your own occasional flubs, or to take responsibility when your child's sad feelings are the reasonable result of something that happened to him or her. Sometimes, no matter how hard it is to accept, parents just don't have control over a situation.

Your job as a parent is to guide and support your child and offer comfort when necessary. You cannot shield him from all bad experiences, nor should you try. Your child will have disappointments and some pain in life, just as you have, and it is your job only to love your child through these tough times and maybe help him to learn from them. It's your job to love the children you have, to enjoy your life and your family, to get through your life as best you can, and to nurture yourself and your family.

Your task as mother is to raise your children to become independent, competent, kind, and reasonably content adults while you are at the same time trying to figure out how to do that, and also living your own life as an adult, as a daughter, friend, life-mate, or worker. Notice that you are not responsible for your children's or your family's happiness, nor is your success or failure measurable in any immediate sense. *If you take your motherhood seriously, this is a very big job.* Yet the best approach to motherhood without guilt is relatively easy: it is simply to try to do what you think is right, as often as possible, to be kind to yourself and others, and to have faith that you are doing a good enough job.

I hope this book will help you do just that.

About the Author

Debra Gilbert Rosenberg, a licensed clinical social worker, is the author of *The New Mom's Companion: Care for Yourself While You Care for Your Newborn*. In addition to her writing, she works as a psychotherapist in a community mental health center, develops and presents workshops and lectures on parenting issues, leads discussion groups for first-time mothers, and teaches sociology classes at Dominican University. She and her family live in Oak Park, Illinois.

Index